ABOUT THE AUTHOR

Steven Colborne is a British-Dutch philosopher, author, and musician. He was born in 1982 in Cambridge, England, grew up in Abingdon near Oxford, and moved to London in 2000 to study. He is a first class BA (Hons) graduate of the University of Westminster and holds a PG Cert in Philosophy and Religion from the University of London.

Colborne is the author of several acclaimed books, including the bestselling *God's Grand Game: Divine Sovereignty and the Cosmic Playground* and the spiritual memoir *The Philosophy of a Mad Man*. In 2012, he established *Perfect Chaos*, an award-winning philosophy and theology blog with several thousand subscribers. He currently lives in South West London.

COPYRIGHT

TEALIGHT BOOKS
London, England
www.tealightbooks.com

The God Articles

ISBN (Paperback): 978-1-9162015-6-9
ISBN (Kindle): 978-1-9162015-7-6
ISBN (EPUB): 978-1-9162015-8-3

British Library Cataloguing-in-Publication Data
A catalogue record for this book is available from the British Library

This book is dedicated to Almighty God

Please, God, remember my suffering and repay me with kindness.

Please, God, remember all of the times that in desperation I begged you for mercy, and be gracious to me.

Show Yourself to be a loving God, Lord, always, because suffering is terrible and happiness is wonderful.

Please, God.

Amen.

THE GOD ARTICLES

STEVEN COLBORNE

CONTENTS

Introduction   xiii

PART I

2012

1. Conversations with Martin (Part 1/2)   3
2. Conversations with Martin (Part 2/2)   13
3. Reflections on Friendship   26
4. Compassionate Justice   28

PART II

2013

5. Artificial Intelligence   33
6. No One is Invincible   35
7. Building a Church for Everyone   37
8. Being Called to Celibacy   39
9. Living in Psychiatric Hospital   41
10. Everything is Sacred   43
11. The Gift of Healing   45
12. Robots and Human Emotions   47
13. Thoughts About the Afterlife   49
14. Tension on the Ward   51
15. There is Always Light Around   53
16. Making Sacrifices   55
17. Everlasting Life   57
18. Prayer for Good Friday   59
19. TUCOAG Opening Prayer Idea   60
20. Prayer for Housing   62
21. Prayer for a Healthy Heart   63
22. A Prayer: 'Let It Be True'   64
23. Prayer to Banish Evil Forces   66
24. Life Goes On...   67

25. God is Merciful   69

26. What can we Learn from Lazarus?   71

27. Holding Onto Hope   75

28. Living with the Question   78

29. Where Next? Some Reflections   81

30. My Peculiar Relationship with Jesus   85

31. Truth Beyond Christianity: There is no Free Will   89

32. May God Grant us Peace!   91

PART III

2014

33. Finding Deeper Meaning in Life's Stresses and Strains   97

34. All is Transparent and Harmonious to His Eye   100

35. Morning Anxiety and Depression   103

36. Exploring Cognitive Behavioural Therapy   106

37. Autogenic Training   108

38. Life After Death   110

39. Pray for a Miracle   113

PART IV

2015

40. A Response to 'Stephen Fry on God'   117

41. Suffering, Death, and the Afterlife   120

42. A Response to Richard Dawkins on the Absurdity of the Crucifixion   123

43. A Prayer of Thanks   126

44. What is the Meaning of Life?   128

45. The Devil Doesn't Exist   130

46. Why I am Getting Baptised   133

47. Understanding the Devil   136

48. My Baptism Today   139

49. He's Just a Prayer Away   142

50. A Few Words About Jesus   144

51. The Importance of Prayer   147

52. Evidence for Jesus' Divinity   151

53. By His Stripes We Are Healed 153
54. Faith Through Suffering 158
55. Deep Fellowship 160

PART V
2016

56. The Bible and Patience 165
57. The Role of Women in Church 169
58. Why is Lent Important? 173
59. The Ten Commandments 175
60. The Grace of God 179
61. Being Held by God 182
62. Christological Conundrums 184
63. Calvinism and Predestination 187
64. Who are the Heretics? 192
65. The Most Serious of Games 196
66. Tony the Alcoholic (a case study) 202
67. Jerry Bridges and God's Sovereignty 205
68. Counselling and Faith 210
69. What is the Holy Spirit? 215
70. My Guilty Americano 221
71. God's Omnipresence and the Incarnation 224

PART VI
2017

72. Do Unbelievers 'Suppress the Truth'? 229
73. Life's Too Short? 231
74. My Favourite Quatrains 233
75. Living the Gospel 236
76. The Bible and Homosexuality 242
77. My Holy Spirit Baptism 248
78. Time is Short 251
79. Two-Day Adventure With God 254
80. Can I Lose my Salvation? 259
81. Some Truths About God 265
82. The Flexibility of God 267

83. Is Everything Subjective? 270

84. Making Plans 273

85. Jesus as Logos 275

86. The Logos as a Person 278

87. The State of It All 281

88. Is it Really Worth it? 284

89. Christian Love 286

90. Lord Over my Life 289

91. Is God Able to Lie? 295

92. Two Vital Questions 297

PART VII
2018

93. Pascal's Wager Discussed 303

94. Must I Love My Enemies? 307

95. Christian Morality and Artificial Intelligence 310

96. From My Heart, to God 312

97. How We Got the Bible 316

98. Unconditional Love 318

99. Everyday Mysteries 321

100. Is Philosophy Important? 324

101. Is Meditation Good For You? 328

102. The Blessing Dilemma 331

103. Geoffrey Parrinder: Interfaith Master 334

PART VIII
2019

104. Debunking the Law of Attraction 339

105. Life: Tragedy or Comedy? 343

106. Your Past Does Not Determine Your Future 346

107. You Never Know (poem) 349

108. Noughts and Ones 351

109. Why Are You Cruel, Lord? 353

110. The Madness of Science 355

111. Humane Prisons 357

112. Mental Illness and the Chemical Imbalance   360
     Myth
113. The Future is Terrifying   364

PART IX
2020
114. The Great Vacuousness of All That I Am and   369
     Ever Will Be
115. Some Words About God   371
116. Why Does God Punish Dreadfully, When   373
     Jesus Teaches Forgiveness?
117. Is Christianity True?   376
118. Hearing from God   382
119. A Guide for Agnostics   384
120. Stream of Consciousness   389
121. A Conversation with Sandra   399

     Also by Steven Colborne   415
     Contact Details and Websites   417

INTRODUCTION

I am delighted to share this collection of articles written between 2012 and 2020 and originally published on my blog, *Perfect Chaos*. The articles in this book have been carefully selected on the grounds that I feel each one contains insights that contribute meaningfully to the fields of philosophy and theology.

The subject matter of the book is quite diverse, and while God is at the heart of almost every article, there are different genres of writing in the book, including discourses, dialogues, prayers and poems, as well as some testimony related to my spiritual life.

In Part 2, there are some articles I wrote during a spell in psychiatric hospital. These are still very much focused on God and spirituality, and I hope they provide an interesting insight into what an experience of that kind is like.

The parts of the book appear by year in chronological order, and the chapters within each part are also arranged in chronological order (with the exception of Part 1, because I liked the idea of beginning the book with a dialogue; a kind of nod to the dialectic style of ancient Greek philosophy). The structure of the book is designed to have the effect of enabling readers to follow the unfolding of events in my spiritual journey as they happened.

Back in 2012, I published a book entitled *The Philosophy of a Mad Man*, which included the story of the most important events in my spiritual journey up until that time, as well as an overview of some of the most important elements of my philosophical perspective. I suppose that, in a sense, *The God Articles* represents the next instalment in the story, demonstrating the evolution of my spiritual journey and philosophical perspective since I wrote that book (although my philosophical perspective has remained largely the same).

Due to the restrictions of being on a tight budget at the time of writing, I was unable to follow my usual process of inviting a proofreader to look over the final draft of the book prior to publication. I said a prayer about this, and God said that I should go ahead and publish the book regardless. This frightens me a little as my grammar is far from perfect, but I have edited the manuscript to the best of my ability. While readers may spot the occasional error in punctuation, I hope I have managed to avoid any errors that could cause confusion in relation to the substance of the ideas I have tried to communicate. If I have slipped up at all in this regard, I sincerely apologise. While I strive for linguistic perfection,

I'm only human, and we all have our quirks of style and our oversights, so please afford me a little grace.

Exploring life's big questions has been the great joy of my life, and I cannot think of a more important thing that one could ever do with their time (aside from, perhaps, praying to God). I hope that my writing in this volume will have the effect of making readers feel excited about the study of philosophy and theology, and I hope readers will find the content refreshing, insightful, and enlightening.

At various points in the book I refer to some of my other published works, and readers will find a list of these near the end of the book.

I'm grateful to God that this book has made its way into your hands, and I thank you from the bottom of my heart for taking the time to read it.

❋ I ❋

2012

CONVERSATIONS WITH MARTIN
(PART 1/2)

19th February 2012

I recently had an email discussion with my good friend Martin (not his real name – he wanted to remain anonymous) which started with the subject of panentheism and grew to incorporate discussion surrounding sacred texts, morality, and a great deal more. I wanted to share a few highlights from our chat, which I hope you will find interesting.

I have separated our discussion into sections, each prefaced with a question that was being considered. I thought that this was the best way to sensibly relay the content of an email discussion that contained many different threads and quoted sections.

Panentheist or pantheist?

Steven:

I don't know if you've ever come across panentheism or pantheism? Panentheism is basically the belief that the whole universe is 'in God' and it's what I believe. The trouble is, Christians tend to believe that some things exist apart from God, like the devil, for instance. I find it impossible to understand how something can exist in opposition to God, who for me created and sustains everything.

Martin:

I would certainly say that what seems to have most in common with what I think (or what I used to think when I used to spend more time thinking about such things) is pantheism, rather than panentheism *[pantheism is the view that the world and God are identical − ed]*. I believe that 'god' is one with nature/the universe rather than a separate creator of the universe. Perhaps my main reason for this is that I struggle to think of something existing outside the universe and time, when I can't (and who can?!) conceive of the vastness of the universe and time as they are.

How are we to understand panentheism?

Steven:

In my view of panentheism, God is creator and, importantly, sustainer. I have a very 'present moment' understanding of God, i.e. the reason why blood is flowing around my body, my hair is growing and my heart is beating, is because God is 'doing' those things. The scientist would of course argue that they are biological processes, but the question then for me is, what is making those processes happen? Can this vast and complex universe be purely mechanical? I don't think so, I think the universe is alive with what I call 'the animating power of God'.

Martin:

I feel the same as this, I agree that 'god' is 'doing' these things, and that god is the 'reason' all things happen – and that scientific mechanical explanations and biological processes can fit in perfectly with this. But how is your above belief panentheism rather than pantheism? Because god is creator? I would like to know what pantheists think about how the world was created? In panentheism, if god exists externally to the universe, is he doing something else too? Or is he just sustaining the universe externally – yet also internally because he is the sustainer?

Steven:

I love your question about 'what else is God doing' other than the universe! It's a little tricky to answer. I think my answer would be that there may be a way in which God exists but is doing nothing, as well as everything, and that there is also the potential within God for infinite creativity that is unexpressed. Perhaps these things make Him more than His creation? (I use the capital 'H' in 'Him' and male gender out of Christian habit!).

Is the universe ordered by a living God?

Steven:

I believe that although the universe is chaotic in certain respects, there is a very definite order to things. Like the way the planets move, and like the way that if you look down at the earth from an aeroplane at motorways and cities everything seems to be ordered. And there are ecological systems, the bees and the honey and flowers and oxygen and light and how all of that works together, that seems to represent order. How does all this order come about? For me, God is 'doing' everything!

Do human beings have a special place in creation?

Steven:

As regards humans having a special place in creation, I'm not sure about that one. I can understand that human beings might have more 'power' (e.g. nuclear weapons, huge cranes, space rockets) and some philosophers would say that we have reason which sets us apart, but are we more valuable than other creatures? I think panentheism would veer on the side of 'no', because God permeates the universe and is therefore in birds as much as humans. But Christianity certainly seems to have a special place for humans, as you suggest. I suppose if the Bible really is the true word of God as many Christians believe then we would have to believe humans have a special place because of the scriptures in Genesis about man having dominion over the other creatures.

Martin:

I think that I disagree with scientists who say that reason sets us apart from other animals. Although I would agree that we have a very well developed capacity to reason, I think that animals also have the capacity to reason, and I also think that we are very similar to other animals in that we obey our instincts and what we have learnt from our past experiences and upbringing, rather than abstract reason far more often than not. So behaviourally I do not think we can wholly separate ourselves from other animals (maybe only in degrees), and thought-wise – we simply do not know what animals think (I think!). So for this reason I don't think I can ever believe that any sacred text is the word of god. We are just attributing human characteristics to god in my opinion.

I think what I am trying to say here that as I believe that there is no distinction in terms of importance between humans and other animals in the universe, anything that humans 'create' (sacred text wise) has no more value truthwise than anything any other animals may attempt to create / communicate. I realise that I may have just provided a good argument against myself in that its seems nigh on impossible that any other animal could create a system of beliefs and communicate it, but I suppose it is logically possible!?

Steven:

I agree in that I think animals also have the capacity to reason. As you suggest, we cannot know, but I see birds making decisions to sit on a branch or swoop for that worm, and I'm not sure how much that differs from our reason. Animals may also have imaginative thoughts. I'm not sure it's simply a matter of brain size, as you get some animals without brains (jellyfish I think?) that live lives of doing and moving and eating just as we humans do.

How important are 'sacred texts'?

Steven:

Is there something special about the Bible? Perhaps. I know that all three times I have been in psychiatric hospital, for reasons that I can't explain, I turned to the Bible for truth and for help. In those dark moments it seemed to provide light and encouragement. Who can explain why I turned to the Bible and why it spoke to me so profoundly at those times? Why has the Bible lasted for two thousand years? Why do Islam, Judaism and Christianity all have scriptures in common, i.e. the Old Testament prophets? Can man alone make these scriptures so globally important?

Martin:

This is the crucial point I suppose. Where I cannot believe that any sacred text, or any human made religion (as I see them) to have really stemmed from god in any way more vital or powerful than anything else that exists in the world, I can completely empathise that a feeling of faith is the only way a person ever could or should believe in one particular religion or text, and that this faith is surely more worthwhile when grounded in a specific experience (or 3!) rather than something that has been taught.

Which religion is correct?

Steven

With a panentheistic view, God has created all religions, therefore how do we pick which one is correct?

Martin:

My immediate response to this, and it must be crucial to our different views, is that humans have 'created' all religions, not god, in my view. Although I would agree that god is and does everything in the universe, and so in that sense has created all religions, in my opinion god has no more created religions that he has created cars. In my opinion, humans have invented cars and religions, though cars and religions are part of god's creation, if you follow what I mean!? And therefore it would be logical in my view that religion has no more value truth wise in informing us about god than cars do.

Steven:

Ah, now this is important, and to me is about the whole question of what God is doing and not doing. You see in my view, God is responsible for all human action, and that goes back to what I was saying about how it is God that makes my hair grow, my blood flow, etc. So I see the world as kind of like a play, wherein we are animated entirely by God. I get the impression you don't see things in quite this way, and believe in free will? I don't believe there is any will aside from God's will, so I don't believe in free human agency. How can God be in all things, and doing all things, and there still be free will? Very interested to get your thoughts on this.

Martin:

Can't god's 'will' be that all beings have free will? As god has free will (though I'm not sure it does – see below) and we are all part of god (god makes our hair grow etc), it seems to me that we can't but have free will – all actions we take are gods actions as we are part of god. It is logically impossible to act against god's will, as our will is gods will. The thing that strikes me as I write this is that I don't believe that god has a will as such, god just 'is'. It may be just a language problem, but whenever we use human attributes when talking about god, it doesn't seem right to me. I don't think god cares whether we have free will or not, and it doesn't care whether we manufacture items, sports or religions – although god is the force that enables us to act/manufacture (and any other verb).

Probably the reason why we seem to agree that god is the motivating force behind everything, and indeed, in my view, is everything, but yet we don't agree on much / anything else, or perhaps even understand quite what the other is getting at (not so surprising given our method of communication!) is that we probably mean different things by 'god'. I don't think god has desires, a will, emotions, requirements, or a 'mind' as such. I think god is nothing like a being that we would recognise. God to me is a force, and not just a force, the force. The force that forces all forces, and would not 'be' otherwise.

How important is Jesus to all of this?

Steven:

In terms of choosing a religion, if Jesus really was the Son of God then I would have to choose Christianity, but the degree of difference between Jesus and other human beings is troublesome in panentheism, because if God is in everything, there is a sense in which we are all sons and daughters of God.

Martin:

I agree with this view – all beings are sons and daughters of god of equal value.

Steven:

But I can still conceive that Jesus may have been different in some way, set apart as unique by God. At Jesus' baptism there was a voice from heaven that said "This is my Son, the beloved, in Him I am well pleased" (Matthew 3:17). What does this mean? Do we have to assume that this was some kind of false vision?

Martin:

To me this is purely a matter of faith, not reason, so I can't comment on it as I don't have religious faith.

Steven:

OK, but to me there is an important question about whether or not to believe these things. Because Jesus' claim to be the Son of God is very significant and has implications for everyone on earth. One still has to ask questions (and reason) about the truth of Jesus' claims, no?

Martin:

I don't believe in the truth of Jesus' claims to be the son of god. Not as being son of god in anyway more significant than all beings are caused by god, and are as such 'sons of god'. So Jesus' claim to be the son of god has no implications as such for me as I don't have faith in this. No Islamic beliefs have any implications for me, and no religious beliefs have any implications for me unless / until I start to subscribe to a religion.

2

CONVERSATIONS WITH MARTIN
(PART 2/2)

2nd March 2012

This is the second part of my email conversation with a friend in which we began by discussing panentheism and then moved on a variety of subjects including free will, the nature of God, morality and ethics, and more.

Each discussion topic is prefaced with a question, which will hopefully make the conversation easier to follow. I realise that the text is a little disjointed in places, and I apologise for this. I have relayed the contents of our email exchange to the best of my ability. I hope that you will enjoy the discussion.

Is truth more important than faith?

Steven:

It's interesting to consider whether 'the truth' is more important than 'faith'.

Martin:

Definitely – I believe this consideration is absolutely paramount.

Steven:

This is something I have struggled with a bit recently. Perhaps there are some things we aren't supposed to understand, and should simply believe? Perhaps that is what Christianity asks us to do, and what if this is right in God's eyes and really is the way to salvation?

Martin:

This seems perfectly sensible in terms of a religious purpose – but it is very difficult to persuade someone without faith to believe in this.

Steven:

...but then there is the history of philosophy, which seems to have been about a search for the truth, so maybe when there are things that we believe to be more rational than a particular belief it is right to go with that. Maybe truth is the ultimate thing worth searching and living for.

Martin:

I wouldn't say that because something has the appearance of being more rational and reasonable then it is right to 'go with that' instead of a religious / faith belief. If you hold a sincerely felt religious belief which is hard (or impossible) to explain using reason, to me this is possibly worth more than a point of argument that has the appearance of reason on its side.

Philosophers can be greater slaves to reason, maintaining their viewpoint no matter what strange conclusion it may lead them to, than a religious person may be a slave to their belief system. And we haven't explained everything away yet using reason (as far as I am aware) so why should reason be held in such esteem?

As you may have noticed, I'm all for arguing against things, but I don't have much positive to offer in terms of what I do believe. I hold out absolutely no hope of establishing anything that I firmly believe in – I doubt I will ever subscribe to a religion unless I have a certain experience, but who knows. But I seriously doubt I will ever subscribe to a purely scientific / reason view either. Basically I have no faith (!) that anything humans can conjure up – whether religious, scientific or philosophic – can hold any perfect (or even near perfect) explanation of the universe. Not that it isn't worthwhile trying...

Steven:

I'm not even sure I believe in reason! I think reasoning seems to be relative. But then we could get into logic and the mathematics of thought and then it would seem like there is reason, as A + B really does lead to C, etc...

Does God have a plan?

Steven:

You seem to be saying you don't have all the answers, and probably won't ever have, and that seems to me to be quite realistic. It seems to be part of God's plan that we don't have all the answers in this life. But as you suggest, you may well have experiences that develop your faith in a certain way at some point, we shall see!

Martin:

I don't believe that god has a plan. I wouldn't say that I had a faith, just a belief (quite possibly unfounded and quite possibly not a true belief) that god exists. Given the inklings I have hopefully given you about what I believe 'god' to be, do you think that I actually believe in god? Because I would say that I do, but I could understand why a religious person would say that I didn't believe in god. But I think what I believe does seem to be in common with pantheism?

Steven:

I really am intrigued about your idea of God. I believe God to be the supreme being with complete free will, who created and is shaping the universe in every moment. I am quite sure that God does have plans, as the vast networks of interactions that take place between things and creatures in the world seem to me to be purposeful, rather than random.

You say God is a force, *the force*, which is quite interesting. That does sound panentheistic and I do agree, in a sense. Maybe where we disagree is that I believe God to be in a sense personal; God is living and able to talk to people, for instance. Do you believe that God is living? Do you believe God can talk to people? Do you believe God makes a decision about whether or not a thunderstorm is going to happen, or whether a person will be born? If the answer to these questions is no, then I'm not sure what you mean by God.

It seems to me that if God is doing everything, as we both seem to agree He is, then that implies that He is doing things in a certain way. If this is the case, then things could be other than they are, if God chose to do differently. Otherwise, in what sense do you believe God is doing everything?

Martin:

My main problem is that I neither agree nor disagree with what you have stated about the nature of god, mainly I just believe that somehow the language you use such as 'plans' 'decisions' 'living' 'talk' to describe god are inconsistent with what god is/does.

I would have to say that I don't think of god as a 'being' as such. I think god is a force – but maybe there's no difference between force and being. The idea of god as a being who makes decisions, communicates with humans etc seems to me to be detrimental / denigrating to god's nature/power. But I agree god created and is shaping the universe. I suppose what I believe is that there is a force who exists and whose nature is beyond the possibility of human cognition and I call this god – but maybe I should call it something else!

Steven:

I'm intrigued to know what the force is doing. Can you describe it in any more detail? For instance, what is the force doing in an apple? (making it grow, presumably). What is the force doing in a table? Is there anything behind the force, making it happen? If not it must be intelligent, right?

Martin:

I would say that the vast networks of interactions that you mention are certainly not random, but I would be very reluctant to call them 'purposeful' either (though of course they serve purposes on a 'lower' level). They are powered by god hence aren't random, but again, the use of the word 'purpose' proves a struggle for me. God could have a purpose in creating the universe, but what would that purpose be, and would we be able to comprehend it? If the purpose has anything in particular to do with humans, then I would be unable to accept it. Why would a force of such immense and incredible power (and I believe these to be denigrating words, but what can we do!) 'care' about creating this universe that is so large and beautiful etc etc – wish I could think of better words – with any kind of 'purpose' specifically for such insignificant, temporary beings as humans?

Steven:

I don't know that we are insignificant or temporary, I rather think we are significant and eternal. Because I believe God 'animates' us, I see that He is taking great care in each moment to unfold our lives. I believe all of creation is 'animated', and so God is taking great care in all of it, making all of the parts interact, giving us thoughts and feelings and actions – it seems as though a lot of work is going into it (although to describe God as working is a bad metaphor as there may well be an ease to the way in which God works as He is supremely powerful).

You ask about what God's purpose might be in creating the universe. Perhaps the whole of creation is God exploring God's nature. If within God are infinite possibilities, then God's creating is like self-expression. Perhaps God is the animator of a grand universal play, and it all exists for God's pleasure?

Martin:

If god does have a purpose (which seems such a human concept to attribute to it) then the chances of the purpose of this whole universe having anything at all to do with humans seems minuscule to say the least. And to my mind, the only 'proof' we have that would suggest otherwise is the existence of texts/religions as written by humans (though of course humans' capacity to create such things is entirely due to the existence of god – in the same way that anything else we have produced is).

Steven:

But surely, if God takes the time and effort to make our blood flow, our hair and nails grow, etc, then that shows tremendous care towards humanity? Why would God create humans unless there was a point to us? Or do you not see God as creating humans, is it more chance that we exist?

Martin:

To answer your questions – for what my answers will be worth (not a lot) – I believe god is living, I believe god can communicate to people (but that it can also communicate to monkeys, ants, weeds, the sea, mountains). I believe god makes thunderstorms happen in the same way that it makes

19

everything happen, so in a sense it does make a 'decision' about this – but not a human style decision!

Likewise for a child being born. And for me there is no more value in god's 'deciding' whether a child is born or not, than god's 'deciding' about anything else at all. So I suppose my answers are not 'no', but not 'yes' in the same way that I presume you would answer 'yes'.

I agree that god is doing everything, and that it is doing them in a certain way, and most certainly agree that things could be other than they are if god 'acted' in a different way.

Steven

Yes, I agree. God has choice in every moment. God can 'intervene' in any situation, although in doing so God is really intervening in God's own action.

If God is a 'force', how does that work?

Martin:

I wouldn't know how to explain what my force is doing in objects, other than to say I believe it is the cause behind, and in, the objects. Also, the force is intelligent in itself, and doesn't have anything behind it making it happen – I suppose it is self causing – hence it feels natural for me to call it 'god'!

Steven:

This seems to relate quite well to my understanding of God – being in and behind all things.

Martin:

As for the type of 'decision' god makes – I think god is the cause of all things and is responsible for all that happens, as the intelligent force. However, I don't think god makes a conscious decision of whether to proceed with a thunderstorm or not each time one occurs – more like thunderstorms are a necessary feature of god's creation. So god is the reason thunderstorms occurs, but I struggle to say it has made a decision each time.

What role does God play in creation?

Martin:

I like the idea of god's creating/creation as being god's self expression – I think this would allow me to say that all of creation is serving no particular purpose, although I doubt you would say this...

I do see god as creating humans, and wouldn't say we, or anything else, is 'chance' – I'd be more tempted to say all of creation has come about as necessary continuations. The main point I am trying to make below is that there is no more value in humans than there is in any other being.

Steven:

I'm not sure what necessary continuations are?

Martin:

Necessary continuations – please refer to my mate Spinoza! I suppose what I mean is that although god is responsible for the existence of humans – and in that sense 'created' us – I don't believe that god created us out of nothing – we are a necessary continuation (or evolution) due to all (or part) of the other parts of god's 'creation'. With god's creation as it is, there could not not have been us, in other words, there must have been us!

Steven:

Your use of the term 'necessary continuations' seems to me to be linked up with evolution, and the idea that God set the world in motion and then it subsequently evolved according to God's laws. I don't know if that's exactly what you believe, but a lot of people do believe that, I think it's called Deism. My problem with Deism is that it takes God out of the everyday, like my current decision to take a sip of coffee. To me God is presently doing this through me, whereas I think to a Deist God is more detached from the present. I'm not sure what a Deist would say God is doing right now!

Martin:

I could sympathise with the idea of Deism, but I wouldn't say that god set up the world and left it. I would probably agree that "the creator does not intervene in human affairs or suspend the natural laws of the universe" (Wikipedia!) but I wouldn't agree that God has 'left' the world. In answer to your question about what god is doing now, I would say that as god exists independently of time, it is both doing everything and nothing – in which case it doesn't make sense to think of god as 'doing' anything at any particular time. I would probably have to say that god has some involvement in your decision to take a sip of coffee – god has certainly made this possible –

but can I really say that and that it is not intervening in your affairs?! I'm not sure! I really think that our language and our concepts restricts so much of what I would say about god.

How does this discussion relate to morality and ethics?

Martin:

I'm keen to find out your thoughts on ethics / morality, which seems to be a natural progression from what we've been talking about. What do you think about good and evil/bad and right and wrong? My understanding of these terms is that they are human inventions – very useful ones – but that that they do not exist. I'll leave it there for now!!

Steven:

Good idea to move on to morality/ethics! Because I believe God to be doing everything, it's difficult to talk about good and bad and right and wrong. Everything has the same source, so how can you distinguish between these criteria? I believe God uses suffering in people's lives as a way of adding to earthly experience. Life is a journey directed by God, and suffering is part of what God chooses for us to experience. My hope is that God never lets the amount of suffering that any individual experiences get too bad, even though I appreciate that suffering can be extremely horrible in certain circumstances.

I do believe that there is a way in which we exercise free will, even though I believe free will is illusory, and that it is really God's will operating in us when we make decisions. But make decisions we do, and therefore there is a way in which we can choose between good and bad action, between harming others or benefiting them. I am not sure at the moment whether I believe the Bible to be God's word, or not. If it is, then clearly it is there for our moral guidance and we should learn the lessons contained in it. I know you don't believe this is the case.

Martin:

I pretty much agree with what you have said about good/evil/right/wrong! It seems that we both deny that good and bad objectively exist. I would also agree about the free will part – we are able to make decisions, and we can attempt to choose between what we believe to be right and wrong, although these are subjective values. I suppose the problem if one does believe the bible to be the word of god, is that then there is such a thing as good and bad (I would say that the bible indicates that there is such thing as 'good' and 'bad'?), and god is telling us the difference between them (again, I'm presuming he does?). Therefore we should apply the guidance he gives in the bible to all aspects of our modern lives, and this, I would imagine, is pretty difficult. Is what I have just said remotely sensical / sensible?! I would add that even if the bible isn't the word of god, and even if right and wrong don't exist, the help these provide are crucial in our attempts to live in the most beneficial way to society and ourselves.

Steven:

In terms of the ethical stuff it surprises me that we are largely in agreement as well! I agree with what you have said about the Bible and its significance if it is or isn't the word of God.

It's something I feel I really need to figure out my stance on, as if the Bible is God's word I need to spend my life studying it! Have you read much of the Bible? I've read all of the New Testament, and Genesis, Exodus and a couple of other books from the Old Testament, there's lots that I haven't read though. I sometimes listen to UCB Bible, which is a radio station where the Bible is read out all day every day. But since I have started to believe myself to be a panentheist, I have stopped reading the Bible, as there is a big question mark over the Bible's significance (as much discussed by us!). I'm not sure whether it's something I will be able to settle in my mind, or whether I will remain in doubt for the rest of my life!

With the Bible there is also the issue of its openness to interpretation. Even if the Bible does give moral guidance, it's still human beings with their radically differing opinions who have to interpret what the Bible says. Christians would normally say they rely on the guidance of the Holy Spirit to show what truth is. I believe in the Holy Spirit in a sense, although I think it is the ever-present spirit of God that permeates everything, whereas for most Christians it seems to be something that comes and goes (i.e. one might or might not be 'filled with the Holy Spirit').

Martin:

I haven't read any of the bible since whatever we may have had to listen to at school, so I am completely unable to talk about its contents! Perhaps I should read some of it, but I've never felt the inclination, any more than I have to read any other religious text.

3

REFLECTIONS ON FRIENDSHIP

5th February 2012

After a very productive 'deep and meaningful' conversation with one of my best friends recently, I started to reflect on the nature of friendship, and a few thoughts emerged regarding what constitutes a healthy friendship. These are my reflections.

There is a place of true connectedness where both friends can be free to be their childlike selves — there is a *zone* where nothing is being suppressed and where all emotions can be expressed without reservation or tension; happiness, sadness, anger, joy, frustration, anxiety, etc. In the zone of pure friendship, much laughter is to be found. Laughter arises quite spontaneously when both friends feel at ease, which is the result of sharing openly. There are no awkward silences in the zone – silences, maybe, but they are comfortable and natural.

The zone can be reached by talking in depth about our experience of being in the present moment. We can ask our friend the question, 'What are you feeling right now?'. It is helpful to explore what is going on in the body. Do I feel nervous? Tense? Fragile? Exploring these things in the context of a friendship helps us to open up, and to feel at ease.

There are normally stories attached to our present moment feelings, which can be expressions of a more complex past. These stories might be of hurt, frustration, or loneliness, and might be the result of years of negative feeling being somehow stored up in the body. To share these stories can be liberating, can help heal broken hearts, and can help friends feel closer together.

In a true friendship there is no need or possessiveness, but instead there is an unconditional love. When you love a person for who they are, you don't need them, you simply want them to be happy.

There never needs to be a reason for a friendship, and it can be damaging to say that your friend is your friend because of such and such a reason, because they make you laugh or because you have the same taste in music. A deep and true friendship will be about so much more that what you have in common with someone — it will be about love.

Friendships are a gift from God and a true blessing. They are to be valued, nurtured, and worked upon, so that hurdles are overcome and a depth of connection is sustained.

4

COMPASSIONATE JUSTICE

4th September 2012

An important question for philosophers in contemporary society is, "How should societies respond to criminal behaviour?"

I do not believe we have free will. Instead, I believe that all events, including the actions of every individual, are under the direct control of God. So God is responsible for criminal behaviour as well as law-abiding behaviour. However, we do have the illusion of free will — in the human dimension of reality we feel that we are making decisions, even if in reality we aren't in control.

Having the illusion of free will means that we can make decisions about how to create laws, how to uphold the law, and how to deal with criminals. We can ask questions about what is logically the best way to create a good society.

It is a fact of human interaction that compassion tends to produce a compassionate response, whereas cruelty tends to create more cruelty. We can see this in the character that children develop in response to the way they are treated by their parents and by other key influencers in their lives.

I believe, therefore, that our approach to justice should be compassionate, focusing always on education, therapy, and rehabilitation, rather than punishment. Change in individuals is always possible because God can do anything, and I believe a compassionate response to criminal behaviour is a better way of affecting positive change than repaying cruelty with more cruelty.

I believe that educating criminals using good reasoning and logic concerning moral action, rather than the deterrent of punishment, is the best way to produce law-abiding behaviour in citizens and create progressive societies. This belief does of course rely on the notion that all human beings are potentially reasonable, which I maintain.

※ II ※

2013

5

ARTIFICIAL INTELLIGENCE

4th February 2013

I realise that the subject of this post is a little out of place on a philosophy blog, but this matter is too important for me to stay quiet about.

I can almost guarantee that everyone reading this post will have had a bad experience with automated "customer service" robots and answering machines. Have you ever been kept waiting ten minutes, twenty minutes, or even thirty minutes to speak to a real human being?

It's a very English or perhaps British thing to complain about our bad experiences with customer services, but the issue I am raising here is much more serious.

Perhaps without knowing it, we are forever attempting to give more and more power to computerised systems and other robotic devices. Facebook, Twitter, the Internet generally, answering machines and cash points are a few examples.

The tech news is always full of "exciting" new inventions – 'The robots are becoming more human, great!', they declare. But if you have ever watched Star Trek or Terminator you will realise that robots with human-like powers can be utterly terrifying. Do we want to be assimilated by the Borg? Need I say more?

I would love for customer services to become human again and for the government to abolish credit and debit cards. I believe we need tight controls on computers and on the Internet to ensure that the power of humans over technology is not compromised.

This is an issue that we must take seriously!

🦂 6 🦂

NO ONE IS INVINCIBLE

5th February 2013

We all suffer. Suffering is part of what makes us human. We can pray all we like, we can beg God for mercy, but the likelihood is, we will still suffer.

There is a famous Buddhist saying, "Life is suffering", which is very bleak when looked at from a certain perspective. But from a somewhat more optimistic viewpoint we might say "Life isn't eternal agony".

We all get depressed, but how often do you thank God that things are not so much worse?

Jesus of Nazareth suffered a terrible crucifixion but was rewarded with a 2000 year reign and a wonderful place in history. So when you are suffering try to think to yourself, "Perhaps my suffering serves a purpose?"

When I pray, I sometimes reach out to all the saints and prophets and holy people and beg God for mercy. I know that the combined suffering of every being on Earth is practically nothing compared to the hellish agony that is possible.

Next time you are feeling depressed or helpless, why not reach out to God with a prayer of thanks? For God chooses to be merciful, despite being omnipotent.

Do you have any idea how lucky we are?

7

BUILDING A CHURCH FOR EVERYONE

6th February 2013

My plan, after I am discharged from psychiatric hospital, is to keep taking my medication and attempt, if the divine wills it to be so, to begin bringing together people of different faiths in order to initiate discussions that may eventually lead to the creation of a new church.

Regular readers of this blog will know that the rough plan for the church is to celebrate the diverse faiths that exist on planet Earth and also to plan for the future of humanity.

I have a postgraduate qualification in philosophy and religion and also a little management experience, and I see my role in the new church as one of listening and coordinating and helping to structure the church in an effective way. My unpredictable mental health issues mean that I might not be actively involved in the day to day operation of the church. My role will be more advisory.

It would be great to bring together a team of volunteers who believe in this vision and begin to get the ball rolling. Anyone is welcome to participate!

If you are interested to know more you can visit the website www.tucoag.org, which is the current online home of the project.

❈ 8 ❈

BEING CALLED TO CELIBACY

7th February 2013

The first thing to point out is that it is indeed an honour to do the will of the divine, even if that means making sacrifices. Amen.

When Jesus suffered in the wilderness for 40 days and 40 nights, he was acting out a sacred part of history, and celibacy is a small calling compared to that kind of suffering.

I will, from now on, only have sex for the purposes of procreation, which means no contraception and no "self-pleasing", if you understand my meaning.

No doubt there will be times when my resolve will be tested, but I was intentionally celibate for a year in the past, despite having a girlfriend, so I know it is possible.

I am very grateful to the divine for this honour, which to me signifies a spiritual calling. How things will pan out I cannot be sure, but if my humble life is pleasing to the divine mind then I am truly and deeply thankful.

I am also happy to wait until I am married before having children. Not being a Christian any longer, I am unsure of the kind of marriage or marriages I will have, but I will pray about it, and we shall see.

9

LIVING IN PSYCHIATRIC HOSPITAL

7th February 2013

This hospital is effectively my home. I eat here, sleep here, wash here, brush my teeth here – these are the kinds of things that define a home, are they not?

Oh, and of course there is the yang of the situation, which is that I have been kicked out of my rented accommodation.

Things could always be so much worse. I could be on the street, sleeping rough, without any privacy. Very little money, cold, etc. I have sampled the homeless lifestyle, just for a few days, and I would not be eager to be in that situation again.

Of course, from a philosophical perspective, it is inner peace that matters. It is possible to be homeless and happy, or a psychiatric patient and happy. Essentially, we must be grateful for what we have, count our blessings, and "keep on keeping on".

In my humble opinion, forgiveness is the most precious teaching of Jesus Christ and of Christianity. If we are fortunate enough to never hold grudges regarding the way we have been treated then we must thank the Lord for blessing us very dearly indeed.

10

EVERYTHING IS SACRED

8th February 2013

Just a quick thought for the day.

Part of our human nature is tiredness. Personally, I don't get bored much, but I hear other people complaining of boredom all the time.

If you are a spiritual person you will know that everything is sacred. Every word we write is sacred. Every sip of each drink is sacred. Every utterance of every clean mouth is sacred.

So if you ever feel a sense of monotony creeping into your daily routine, why not pause for a moment, be still, and appreciate the beauty in simple things. Like the touch of your fingers on materials. Like the magic of electricity. Like the taste of a hot drink.

I may be celibate but I know that if someone gave me just a peck on the cheek today I would really appreciate it.

Amen.

⚜ II ⚜

THE GIFT OF HEALING

9th February 2013

Throughout history certain fortunate individuals have been blessed with the ability to heal others. Jesus is the obvious example, along with other saints and prophets and holy people.

It seems to me that I may have been blessed with that kind of a spiritual gift. I am able to empathise with people's suffering because, in a sense, I have been through what they've been through. When I meet with people who are suffering physical or emotional pain, sometimes the divine being makes those people whole and healthy again as I interact with them. This has happened on various occasions.

I am profoundly grateful if this perception is correct, and the divine being is indeed using me in this way.

I believe the divine being appreciates suffering very much, and I believe one of my purposes in this life time has been to suffer on behalf of other people. In the same way people pray to Jesus to end their suffering, it is possible that maybe one day people will reach out to the divine being through me, Steven, and beg for mercy.

Of course, all of this could be a mere figment of my imagination, or perhaps a symptom of psychosis? All that we can really do is wait and see what happens.

12

ROBOTS AND HUMAN EMOTIONS

9th February 2013

Firstly, I'm really grateful if you're reading this. Psychiatric hospital can be a little lonely at times and it definitely lifts my spirits to know a few people are taking an interest in what I have to say.

I was thinking this morning about fear. It is very human to feel fear. It isn't the most pleasant of emotions (neither is it the most unpleasant) but it is very human.

If we are heading towards a future where computers and machines have a significant role in our lives then we must be absolutely sure that they are unable to experience fear and other human emotions. I believe that emotions are a kind of power humans and other animals have and they play an important role in the power structure of our humble planet.

If robots could experience fear and other emotions they would be too powerful. They might use those emotions to subdue or suppress us and it is not impossible to imagine that we could become their slaves. That kind of scenario is truly terrifying.

Perhaps, if you are praying this weekend, you might ask the divine to please keep us humans safe from advances in technology that could compromise our power and freedom on Earth.

What are you doing in your life to ensure technology isn't beating you or us?

13

THOUGHTS ABOUT THE AFTERLIFE

11th February 2013

To be honest, the nature of the afterlife is a complete mystery to me. It seems to be part of our human nature that we can only speculate on the afterlife during this life.

I do, however, have a faint vision of what the afterlife might be like. I believe that angels and other spiritual beings do exist. I also believe there is a place we might call heaven, where there is peace and happiness in abundance.

Could it perhaps be the case that the afterlife is a kind of mirror image of our earthly lives, in many respects, and yet without much (or maybe even any) suffering?

It is also possible that a kind of hell exists. Heaven and hell have been spoken about in philosophy for thousands of years. So we should never be so arrogant as to assume we are definitely going to heaven. I can honestly say that the idea of hell terrifies me; we can hardly imagine the horrors that are possible.

This whole discussion serves to underline the spiritual aspect of our existence, and how our human lives are just a fleeting moment in eternity.

❧ 14 ❧

TENSION ON THE WARD

11th February 2013

There's a fairly dark mood on the ward at the moment. I won't go into details but suffice to say I have been on the receiving end of some rather aggressive anger issues.

I'm doing fine, luckily. Years of psychotherapy and a general education in life's ups and downs have taught me to hold my nerve in times of uncertainty, and to say a prayer and go with the flow.

Defending our peace, and our self-esteem is sometimes a difficult thing to do and we are very blessed if we escape unharmed when aggressors attack. We should respect that the feelings of others are part of the divine plan, even when they are aggressive, and we should pray for mercy for our enemies as well as our friends.

I just want to say thank you to the divine being for not making me suffer more. I realise that I am very blessed, as we all are blessed not to suffer more. I may or may not have had my fair share of suffering in this life time, but whatever happens, things could always be so much worse.

If you feel like saying a prayer for my swift discharge from psychiatric hospital I would really appreciate it.

15

THERE IS ALWAYS LIGHT AROUND

23rd February 2013

A dear friend once told me, in a time of need, "There is always light around".

Isn't it the beautiful truth that when our lives are full of darkness and woe, there is, so often, a twist of fate, and a lightness of being arrives to displace our misery with a brighter mood?

The word that springs to mind is 'mercy'. For there is no doubt that any unhappy situation could persist for weeks, months, years, decades, or even centuries. But so often, the divine being chooses to bring mercy to our darkness, and once again give us a precious optimism to displace our misery.

If the divine being is infinitely wise and infinitely powerful, then in times of misfortune, there is always hope.

Today, I praise the divine being for the tender mercies in my own life, and I trust, as much as I can, that a plan is being worked out for my life with great care and intricacy.

Remember, when you're feeling low: There is always light around.

❀ 16 ❀

MAKING SACRIFICES

12th March 2013

There are times when, in the furtherment of the divine cause, we have to make sacrifices.

We are human beings with real emotions, and we are empathic creatures, which means we feel each others' pain.

Sometimes, if someone around us is going through some challenging emotional experiences, we will pick up on that, and feel what they are feeling, through empathy.

In this situation, our personal sense of space and freedom may be compromised. We might have to "lie low" for a few hours, a few days, or even a few weeks, until the emotional disturbance has passed.

During these times, it is important not to become the victim. We must keep a clear head and a clear heart, carry on, say a prayer, and believe in our personal goals and the divine plan for our lives.

Everything that happens in the entire universe is an expression of the divine will, and to acknowledge that is to have faith.

In times of trouble, why not say a prayer asking that everything might unfold in accordance with the divine will?

✻ 17 ✻

EVERLASTING LIFE

12th March 2013

I have been meditating on the scripture John 3:16 which says, "For God so loved the World that he gave his only begotten Son, that whosoever believeth in Him should not perish, but have everlasting life."

Those two magical words, 'everlasting life', what does that phrase mean to you?

I believe death is a fear that hangs over all our lives, even though really it is suffering we are afraid of rather than death itself.

But what if this consciousness, this aliveness that I am experiencing, would really last forever, uninterrupted by death? That is a profound thought.

If Jesus is generous enough to bless our lives and accept us into his kingdom once our earthly lives are over, then we have nothing to fear! Except for the devil, of course, who will persistently try to interrupt God's plans.

Have you meditated on the significance of John 3:16 in your own life?

❧ 18 ❧

PRAYER FOR GOOD FRIDAY

30th March 2013

Oh my Lord, my Saviour, my King, what words can express the tragic glory of your passion, which we remember today?

You came down from heaven, Lord, you lived a blameless and sinless life, and then you died in agony, oh God, in order that I might be forgiven; such a precious gift that I can barely comprehend.

Lord, as I kneel humbly at your feet, please hear my prayer today. Please help me to know that your terrible suffering - the crown of thorns, the lashes, the humiliation, the nails, the agonising pain − served the most important purpose in the history of man.

By your wounds I am healed. I can claim a life of blessing and abundance because of you, Lord Jesus. From the bottom of my heart I thank you for your sacrifice. Amen.

19

TUCOAG OPENING PRAYER IDEA

1st April 2013

What follows is an idea for a prayer that could begin a service in a new multi-faith church of the future (The Universal Church of Almighty God).

We are assembled today in the presence of Almighty God, the one true God of all the religions of planet Earth.

Lord, please help us to look beyond our differences and worship you in unity, love, and peace.

[all kneel]

As we bow humbly at your feet, Lord God, Allah, Brahman, we call upon the great prophets of Earth, Muhammad (peace be upon him), Abraham, Moses, Jesus (known to many as the Son of God), and all the prophets and saints and the whole heavenly host, to hear our prayers and bless us with their divine wisdom and love today.

Almighty God, you are infinitely strong, wise, and powerful, and we are lowly, weak, and frail. Lord, have mercy on our souls. We, your faithful believers, are terrified of your anger, and above all we beg you for mercy and peace.

We humbly call upon the power of your spirit to fill this place today and to guide us as we seek to glorify your holy name.

If it pleases you, Lord, and if you are willing, please make this church, and our planet, places of friendship and brotherly love, rather than conflict and hatred. Most merciful God, please take away our anger, our pain, and our selfishness, and make us strong in our love for you, as we thank you for everything always, and we say together...

Amen.

❧ 20 ❧

PRAYER FOR HOUSING

2nd April 2013

O most merciful Lord, you are my shelter. Your love surrounds my thoughts and houses my heart. When the storms arrive, your promises protect me. Your salvation is the bed where I lay my head.

Above all, heavenly father, I seek spiritual peace, but my earthly body aches for a safe haven – a dwelling I can call my own.

Lord, if it pleases you, and if you are willing, grant me a humble abode where I can have peace and sleep and rest.

In Jesus' mighty name, Amen.

21

PRAYER FOR A HEALTHY HEART

3rd April 2013

O most merciful Lord, I reach out to you today, frail wretch that I am, seeking comfort in my earthly body. My heart has known such generous love from you, father, but through my life's trials has become weak and in need of repair.

Oh mighty, sovereign, glorious Lord of all, though I am not worthy, I beg of you, take pity on me and restore my heart this day. Please, oh omnipotent ruler, bless me with a holy temple of a body and the health to continue my earthly ministry and service to you.

In the name of your dear Son Jesus and His precious wounds I pray,

Amen.

✣ 22 ✣

A PRAYER: 'LET IT BE TRUE'

4th April 2013

Lord, please, let it be true.

That the death of your Son is my salvation,

Lord, let it be true.

That the agony of the cross was not in vain,

Lord, let it be true.

That by His wounds we are healed,

Lord, let it be true.

That evil has been overcome,

Lord, let it be true.

That I might have a life of abundance,

Lord, let it be true.

That no one need suffer again like you did, Lord,

Please, let it be true.

❧ 23 ❧

PRAYER TO BANISH EVIL FORCES

4th April 2013

Heavenly father, thank you for the great victory over evil that your cross represents.

Most merciful Lord, thank you that the cross is the ultimate weapon against my enemies, and that no evil force, treachery, deceit, or malice that would attack this holy temple will ever succeed.

Cover my life with the blood of Jesus, oh Lord, and protect me from any evil plot that would seek to rob me of the peace of Christ.

May my saviour's suffering be a crushing blow against the enemy in every single area of my life, and I thank you and praise you, heavenly father, for IT IS FINISHED!

In Jesus' mighty name I pray. Amen.

❦ 24 ❦

LIFE GOES ON...

5th April 2013

My dear friends,

I must first offer you an apology because it has been several weeks since I last posted. I am still in psychiatric hospital and circumstances have dictated that I have had very limited internet access and some personal troubles that have prevented me from sharing with you for a while.

You may notice that I have uploaded some Christian prayers that I have been writing while in hospital. I have had a resurgence of my Christian faith and am once again recognising the importance of Christ in my life as my lord and saviour.

This is not to disregard my criticisms of Christianity, as expressed on this blog, which still hold some validity in my mind. I am a Christian but I still believe in the panentheist perspective that says all is 'in God', and indeed, all *is* God, which my regular readers will be familiar with.

This blog was made private for a couple of weeks recently while I gathered my thoughts, but the gates are open once again and I would be delighted for you to have a read of my recent posts and leave your comments on any of my articles, past or present.

Thanks so much for reading.

25

GOD IS MERCIFUL

11th April 2013

Dear friends,

I'm happy to say I am now out of psychiatric hospital and living in the community again. The Lord has been very generous to me, blessing me with a lovely room in a great location. I can't quite believe my luck! This is surely an answer to prayer.

I apologise once again for the lack of updates recently, and also that the blog was made private for a couple of weeks. I was in two minds about whether to carry on with the blog at one stage and making it private seemed wise while I was deciding what to do.

Now I'm out of hospital (which is very refreshing indeed; I was first admitted before Christmas and it is now April) I have a chance to think about the future again. I am feeling more positive about keeping an online presence, and I hope to continue updating this blog and working on several books that I have already started.

When I become unwell, it's hard to know what is fantasy (schizophrenia gives you some funny ideas about reality!), and what is real. I sometimes have lofty ambitions and in the coming weeks I will have to re-assess where I'm at and what I can realistically achieve in this new season of my life.

One thing is clear at the moment. I need Jesus Christ in my life! And I need to keep attending church to stay focused on spiritual matters rather than earthly concerns. Above all, I want to be a good, Godly, generous person and I want to leave a positive impression in the world as I go about my business. I am praying that I can achieve this and I have faith that the Lord will help me.

Peace and blessings to you! Thanks for reading.

26

WHAT CAN WE LEARN FROM LAZARUS?

15th April 2013

Being out of psychiatric hospital and living back in the community is a real blessing. I am lucky to have a roof over my head in a nice house with friendly housemates and a clean bright room, praise God!

As I settle into my new home I am endeavouring to make plans that will make my life fruitful, Godly, and fulfilling. With this in mind I ordered a One Year Bible from Amazon recently and it arrived today. If you don't know what this is, it is basically the whole Bible divided up into 365 daily readings, each day containing a reading from Psalms or Proverbs, an Old Testament reading, and a New Testament reading. It's a great way to focus the mind on regular Bible study without causing one to feel daunted.

Today's New Testament reading was 'The Rich Man and Lazarus' from the book of Luke. The story essentially goes like this. There was a rich man who lived in luxury every day, and a beggar called Lazarus who lived as a homeless person at the gate of the rich man's house. Lazarus lived in poverty, eating only the crumbs that fell from the rich man's table. The earthly existence of these two men is in stark contrast.

We are told that both men eventually passed away, and the poor man went to heaven and the rich man went to hell. The rich man was in agony in hell and started to think of his family who were still alive on earth. He spoke to Abraham, who was in heaven with Lazarus, and asked that Lazarus be sent to his family to warn them of the torments that he was suffering after living his luxurious life. He hoped that they might be saved from similar torment.

The passage made me think about how I live my own life. In my own philosophical writings I have discussed the possibility that perhaps Almighty God, in His mercy, is a fair God. By fair, I mean that maybe God allots a similar amount of suffering to everyone, if we take into consideration life before birth and after death. So maybe those suffering a lot in this life find mercy in the next, and vice versa.

I suppose the passage about Lazarus is a warning. If we feel richly blessed in this life, we must be very careful. For a start, we must not take our riches for granted, and we must always be seeking to help others by giving what we have away. We must have compassion on those who are homeless and needy, and not store up riches on earth. After all, an eternity in hell after death is no doubt far worse than living an earthly life of poverty.

The book of Matthew says, "Do not store up for yourselves treasures on earth, where moths and vermin destroy, and where thieves break in and steal. But store up for yourselves treasures in heaven, where moths and vermin do not destroy, and where thieves do not break in and steal." (Matthew 6:19-20) And in Matthew 19:24 we read the following: "Again I tell you, it is easier for a camel to go through the eye of a needle than for someone who is rich to enter the kingdom of God."

It is true that as Christians we can claim a life of abundant blessing because of the cross and what Jesus did for us. But I believe that our abundance should be spiritual rather than material. We must always use our resources to help other people, and we should embrace poverty and respect those who are disadvantaged in society.

My prayer today is that the Lord would direct me in matters of richness and poverty. I pray that I might use all of my resources to be a blessing to others, and never cling to my worldly possessions. As a start, I am going to consider selling a lot more things on Ebay, giving away clothes, and using my savings wisely. I am already donating to five charities each month, and I give money to the church regularly as well. I recently spoke to a pastor at my church and suggested that all the pastors should buy their clothes from charity shops in order to set a good example.

I am sure there is much more I can do, and I will pray to the Lord for guidance.

Do you consider yourself to be rich? Are you taking steps to avoid suffering a similar fate to the rich man in the story?

27

HOLDING ONTO HOPE

3rd May 2013

There is no doubt that when my life is focused on Jesus, and I am engrossed in the Bible and in fellowship with my Christian friends, my life takes on a new dimension; a graceful, glorious dimension. I am absolutely convinced that there is great power in the name of Jesus, and I have witnessed that power again and again in my life.

Despite these truths, at the moment I am suffering from a kind of spiritual insecurity. I want to believe, so very much, but there is an intellectual part of my being that is causing me to doubt some of the fundamental tenets of the Christian faith. I have written about my problems with the faith elsewhere on this blog, and there is no need to repeat them here.

At times like these I just fall on my knees and beg God to reveal His truth to me. It is the most important and rewarding thing in the world to have a relationship with God, and my fervent desire is that I would not do anything to compromise that relationship and risk God's anger.

There may be aspects of the Christian faith that never make sense to me (from an intellectual standpoint) and I suppose the battle I am facing is faith versus intellect. When I think about the power of the cross and the love that I have experienced from the Lord it makes me quite sure that faith must win this battle.

But how can I stop the intellectual doubts from resurfacing and interfering with my Christian walk? It terrifies me that whenever I build spiritual momentum in my life my doubts and questions may resurface and rob me of my peace.

My prayer today is this:

Heavenly Father, most glorious ruler of all, thank you for the peace and blessing that I enjoy in my life.

Help me, most merciful Lord, to live a life based on faith in you, and reveal to me your truths so that they might surround me and stabilise me, and so that I might live in them all my days.

Help me to know what I must know in order to be held in your favour, and help me to rebuke and dismiss any spirit that seeks to rob me of your peace – the peace that surpasses all understanding.

Oh mighty, sovereign, and eternal Lord, give my faith a solid foundation and an unshakable certainty, so that I need not wrestle with doubts and troublesome questions in the future.

Lord Jesus, I offer my life to you, and I say strengthen me, renew my mind, save me from sin, help me to understand, conquer my struggles, and keep me in your peace.

I beg of you, Heavenly Father, please accept this prayer. In the mighty name of Lord Jesus I pray. Amen.

❧ 28 ❧

LIVING WITH THE QUESTION

17th May 2013

Anyone who has read my blog in any depth will recognise that there are two important components to my beliefs about God and the world. On the one hand, there is my panentheist attitude that sees God in everything as the 'cosmic animator' – responsible for everything that happens in existence. On the other hand, there is my Christian faith, which acknowledges Jesus as Lord and is the focal point of my prayer life and my faith.

There is a struggle that goes on in my life every day as I try to reconcile the differences that these two strands of thought and belief present.

It's a simple predicament:

If God is in control of everything that happens, then how am I to understand free will which is central to the Bible and to Christian thinking?

I do not feel that I can be a fully committed Christian with this dilemma filling my thoughts each day. And yet I love to pray and feel I must, and I believe in the life, death, and resurrection of Jesus.

I have probably been frustrating my Christian friends as I have agonised over this dilemma for several years. I recently spoke with an Anglican priest about it and he wasn't able to provide a satisfying solution. Indeed, it seems that no one that I talk to (Christian or not) can reconcile this problem for me. No books that I have read or lectures that I have listened to have helped me to settle the dilemma.

It seems to me that I am going to have to live with the dilemma. That doesn't make life easy – I am "not quite a Christian", which is not a generally acceptable position among my Christian friends who are mostly very evangelical. I don't feel I can preach the gospel with any gusto having the problems with Christianity that I do. And the pull of what I believe is the truth about God is strong enough to keep me believing that the panentheistic vision of God that I espouse is right.

The best advice that I have received on this matter actually came from my own father. We were sat in a park talking about Christianity and as I explained my predicament he suggested I might have to "live with the question". I think that for now, at least, that is good advice.

I can't imagine my life without prayer as a major component and I expect I will always reach out to God to give thanks and praise and to offer supplications. Jesus will remain a hugely important figure in my life, even if I can't commit to His teaching in the same way as my Christian friends. Living with the question at least gives me some peace of mind and I am open to the possibility that God, who is infinite, may reveal new truths to me in the future.

I have almost finished writing my second book which discusses my thinking around these issues in a lot more depth. I hope that the book will help others to gain insights into my struggle, which will in turn enrich their own spiritual journeys.

It is a good thing to seek the truth, and I hope and pray that God loves me for my struggle.

29

WHERE NEXT? SOME REFLECTIONS

17th June 2013

I have been posting regularly on this blog for about a year and a half. My intention at the outset was to convey my views about the God/world relationship in relation to all of the key questions that philosophically minded people ask. I feel that now, having written two books (one published and one on its way) and a few dozen blog posts, I have achieved what I set out to accomplish. I don't think that there is any crucial philosophical question that I have not attempted to tackle in my writing over the last two years.

So the question is, where next? I feel that it's time to put my thinking cap on and to consider how to use the remainder of my life in a meaningful way. God only knows how long I've got left in this world — a few days or a few decades — but I want to make a positive contribution to life on Earth if at all possible.

One thing that will keep me busy is promoting my books. I have experienced first hand how difficult it is to gain recognition as a self-published author. But I believe in my writing and that it is a worthwhile endeavour trying to reach as many people as possible with my blog and my books. So I need to keep pushing for exposure and collaborating with people who can help me to reach a wider audience. In truth, I feel as though I have something important to offer the world in my writing. I believe that God has given me some unusual insights and that the most important purpose of my life, for now at least, is to communicate those insights with others.

I truly believe that the panentheistic vision of the world that I espouse in my writing is the ultimate truth and has the power to break through religious dogma and help lead people to a deeper understanding of reality. I have studied philosophy and religion and explored our planet's spiritual paths in some depth but I have never felt as certain as I do these days that I have landed upon God's truth (or, should I say, the truth about God and the world). I will always enjoy engaging in philosophical discussions with others about my beliefs, and maybe it is a significant part of my destiny to do so.

In any case, I feel as though the time is approaching for me to move into a new phase in my life. I need a new challenge that inspires and excites. I need a way forward that will give my life meaning.

I know it won't always be easy, whatever I decide to do. I have a diagnosed mental illness and I am living in supported housing. I have to take medication which has troublesome side effects and I also have an anxiety disorder that inhibits my life. Nevertheless, I will strive to be productive and structure my life in such a way as to allow me to work on projects and gain satisfaction through them.

There was a time when I was a committed Christian and would have loved to have become a pastor. But after studying and reflecting and reading the Scriptures I found too many theological problems with the Christian faith and it would be wrong for me to pursue that line of work now. That said, I would love to work in a field that is related to philosophy and spirituality as these subjects remain the great passions in my life. Can you recommend any jobs that might be suitable for my interests?

I suppose a dream come true would be to be a pastor in a multi-faith church of the future. But this is a church that I have written about and envisioned but that has no reality at present. If only I could find the right people to work with in order to make this happen! On the other hand, in truth I am a very shy and anxious person, so I'm not sure how well pastoral work would suit me. For the right church or organisation, however, I might be willing to take on the challenge.

Anyhow, first things first, and for now I must focus on completing and publishing my second book, which will have the title 'Ultimate Truth: God Beyond Religion'. The book draws from and expands upon many of my earlier blog posts and I really do believe it is an important book for philosophy. I will be working with SilverWood Books on the publication of the book which should be available by the end of the year. I hope that you will read it!

Thank you for reading my blog and for being a part of this journey with me, I really appreciate it.

30

MY PECULIAR RELATIONSHIP
WITH JESUS

21st August 2013

Every Sunday I get on the 44 bus from Garratt Lane in South West London and make the 30 minute ride through Battersea and across the river to London Victoria. My final destination is Westminster Cathedral, which is just a short walk from Victoria station. During the bus journey I have my iPod on 'shuffle' and get a mixture of Christian music (some hymns and some gospel), rock and metal, and contemporary electronic music in my headphones. The journey tends to go smoothly and quickly (particularly if the music is good), and I am always surprised by how short the final stretch through Belgravia to Victoria station is once the bus has crossed the river at Chelsea Bridge.

It might seem surprising that despite considering myself a non-Christian, I still choose to visit a cathedral every Sunday. After all, Westminster Cathedral is a Catholic building, indeed, it is the centre of Catholic worship in England. Well, the truth is, I feel a real sense of God's presence in the place, despite not being a Christian. There are no religious buildings corresponding precisely to my beliefs, and Westminster Cathedral (along with other Christian churches) does at least offer the right kind of atmosphere for me to pray and reflect and have some 'God time'.

They do of course hold mass in the cathedral, but I don't attend. I did feel inclined to join in a service one Sunday a few weeks ago, but after only a few minutes the content of the liturgy made me feel deeply uncomfortable, and so I quietly put down my prayer books and wandered out to the aisles of the cathedral, where everyone is free to pray to God quietly and in their own way. What made me leave the service? Well, I simply cannot relate to the Christian idea that we are all sinners, and apologising for sins doesn't make sense to me. This is because I believe that God is responsible for every-thing that happens in the cosmos and in our lives; we do not have free will. I have written about this extensively on this blog on and in my books, so there's no need to go into the subject in depth here.

Along the aisles of the cathedral there are chapels dedicated to important religious figures and saints. Everywhere there are metal racks holding dozens of candles, and visitors are invited to light a candle, perhaps in memory of a loved one (and in exchange for a small donation). The atmosphere is solemn and sacred and very beautiful.

My favourite part of the cathedral is an area called the Blessed Sacrament Chapel where there is a statue of a figure who I presume is Jesus holding out his arms. Below the statue is an area where visitors can sit on wooden chairs or kneel to pray. There are only 8 or so chairs so the area feels very private. People often walk up to the statue and touch the figure's bare feet or robe, presumably to absorb some of Jesus' healing power. This feels like a distinctly Catholic thing to do.

When I am kneeling in the Blessed Sacrament Chapel I pray about all kinds of things. Rather than centring my prayers around forgiveness, as Christians do, my own prayers tend to beg God for mercy in terms of the way He treats us. I always pray especially for those who are suffering the most, and I always pray for people in hospital and people in prison and people who are homeless. After each prayer session I light a candle for a particular group of people who I feel have suffered greatly, whether holocaust victims, disabled people, the homeless, or another group.

During my prayer time in the Blessed Sacrament Chapel I often feel God prompt me to reach out to Jesus. And I do. Although my understanding of who Jesus is doesn't equate to the Christian understanding, I still acknowledge Jesus as a special person in God's eyes and a very important spiritual figure. I pray to Jesus for His friendship and ask for His love and support and intervention in my life's circumstances. This goes to show how important I feel Jesus is, even though I'm not a Christian. I really sense how much God loves Jesus, and it warms my heart to think that Jesus might be my friend. I often go up and touch the statue myself, and then I touch my heart, hoping for healing in my own life.

My relationship with Jesus is peculiar because I don't believe as a race we are in need of salvation from sin, which is what Christians generally believe. I don't believe we have free will. God is responsible for everything that happens in our lives. And because we don't have free will, we can have done nothing to deserve the wrath of God, or to warrant the need for salvation. Therefore, I cannot accept much of what Christianity teaches. But I do accept that Jesus is obviously a very important person in God's eyes, so I feel drawn to respect Him and to reach out to Him, and to read with care what is said about Him in the Bible.

When I leave Westminster Cathedral each Sunday I have a feeling of being refreshed, and it is as though a small weight has lifted from my shoulders. I have entrusted my woes and worries into God's care, and I have faith that God will have received my prayers and will look after me and care for me in the coming week.

I have great faith, but it is not Christian faith. It is a faith that God is in control and has the power to unfold my destiny in whatever way He chooses.

31

TRUTH BEYOND CHRISTIANITY:
THERE IS NO FREE WILL

11th September 2013

The first thing to make clear is that I have every respect for Christians, Muslims, Jews, Hindus, and people of all faiths and no faith. Our beliefs, whatever they are, are God-given. It is even correct to say that God gives atheists their unbelief, as strange as that may sound.

But the purpose of this article is to explain why I have moved on from Christianity to a new spiritual understanding that isn't easily categorized. I am close to being a panentheist, which means, literally, "all in God", but that term doesn't capture my beliefs entirely accurately.

In a nutshell, I believe that God's being permeates everything, everywhere, all of the time. I refer to God as The Cosmic Animator because I believe that all activity in the universe, including human activity, is willed and directed by

God. There is no free will! When I write it is God writing through me, and when you speak it is God speaking through you.

If this sounds strange then consider this for a moment: What is making our hearts beat? What is making our blood flow and our eyes blink? What is causing thoughts to arise in our minds? Clearly, there is a force or power making these things happen, and that force or power is God, or the divine, or the supreme being, or whatever you might like to call the Almighty One.

A view contrary to this is that of Christians. Christians believe we have free will, which means we do what we choose independently of the divine will. But in my humble opinion this cannot be possible. If God (or the divine) is omnipresent (everywhere) as most Christian theology supposes, then there is no atom anywhere in the universe that is not under direct divine control. God, therefore, is doing everything.

In reality, there is no freedom to respond to divine commandments, as Christians, Muslims, and Jews, suppose. There never was a "fall" away from God, as Christians believe. If God is omnipresent, these things are impossible, and we must also conclude that there is no devil-like being in competition with God – if the devil exists, he is also under God's control.

32

MAY GOD GRANT US PEACE!

29th December 2013

As I sit alone in my bedroom, I am aware of how quiet this house is at the moment. It's a five bedroom property, but three tenants have moved out in recent months and have not yet been replaced. It is wonderful to be able to enjoy the peace and quiet of a near-empty house, the only distractions being the hum of my mini-fridge and the occasional sirens of police and ambulances in the neighbourhood.

I am especially grateful for the peace today as I am in a thoughtful and reflective mood. Perhaps it's the time of year, but in any case I am really appreciating having the opportunity to think things through. As I sit quietly, thoughts arise about who I am, what I am doing, what I have achieved, and where I am headed.

In a certain moment, I am aware that my life almost seems to make sense. My spiritual journey, my mental illness, my studies, and my career – all of this seems meaningful and coherent when viewed from a certain perspective. The two books that I have written in the last two years; these would not have been possible without my own unique passage through life.

I am proud of the books that I have written, even if I don't always see things in this light. They offer a truthful perspective of my life's journey and my beliefs, and they convey all of the most important things about me as a person. I may only be 31 years old, but I feel as though I have lived a life that is full.

The only problem is – and I have referred to this in recent posts on this blog – I have reached a kind of 'full stop'. I have achieved what I have wanted to achieve (mainly with my writing), and despite the fact that I have not achieved commercial success with my books, I find myself satisfied that I have done all I can with this little life of mine.

I would love to reach a wider audience with my writing, but I no longer have the motivation or confidence to keep pushing. I am a sensitive soul, and I don't think I could cope well with any negative publicity if I did reach a much wider audience. Also, I am lacking in the drive to undertake promotional activities such as interviews and in-store promotions. All of this is too stressful for my fragile mind to cope with!

The one thing that I crave above all else these days is peace. And peace is a very hard thing to find in this lifetime – it is certainly not won by fame and fortune, of that I am quite sure.

So, in 2014 I will be grateful if I have peace in my life. Peace to enjoy a sunny day in the park, peace to be free from stress, peace to be alone and not lonely. This is my last great ambition, and whether I find it in life or death I do not mind.

When I pray these days I simply beg for mercy. Mercy that I might not suffer any more and mercy for all those who suffer so terribly in this world. May God grant us peace!

Amen.

III

2014

33

FINDING DEEPER MEANING IN LIFE'S STRESSES AND STRAINS

7th January 2014

It seems that stress is a part of life for everyone. Yet I believe it needn't be that way. The universe is sustained and animated by an all-powerful God – the same God who beats our hearts, flows our blood, and causes thoughts to arise in our minds. The same God that causes us to grow from nothing into babies, into children, then adults.

The God who creates and sustains us is in control of all our worries, and all our stresses. I am certain that if our God decided it should be so, all our worries could be gone in an instant, and forever. I often pray to God to take away my stresses and worries and to let me have the enduring peace that I suppose we are thinking of when we say the word 'heaven'.

But despite my prayers, the stresses and worries still come each day, and it seems certain that there is no enduring peace to be found in this lifetime for any of us. It is of course true that the stresses and strains could always be so much worse. In any given day, there are always lots of things to be thankful for.

I can only imagine what God's reasons are for causing stress to all human beings, century after century, for thousands of years. It must please God in some way to make us suffer, otherwise He would simply grant us all the peace that we crave. He could do that – create a heaven on earth – if He so wished.

I suppose we have to hang on to the hope that God knows best. God has His reasons for the suffering that we endure. This is hard to fathom, however, as suffering seems to be so needless. Why can't we just have peace *now*?

In my book *Ultimate Truth: God Beyond Religion* I speculate two main reasons why God might wish for us to suffer. Both reasons stem from the idea that God Himself suffers. Firstly, if God is all that exists (which I believe is the case: everything is an expression of God), then God is completely alone. God can create anything He chooses, but all of His creations remain a part of the one God. There is never anything separate from God with which God can interact. God has no choice but to be alone for all eternity. There might be a kind of agony in that.

Secondly, life never has an ending for God. There is no rest from being alive. God has to stay entertained for all eternity!

Perhaps there is a kind of agony in that as well. These are two ways in which I suppose God might suffer.

If we imagine a God who suffers terribly, then it is perhaps a little easier to understand our own suffering. It is possible that we are created to experience different aspects of the divine being. Perhaps God makes us suffer to give us a taste of what ultimate reality is like for Him.

Maybe, buried deep within the stresses and worries of our daily lives, there is a deeper meaning to our suffering. If bliss and agony are both experienced by God, then perhaps it is only fair that we get a taste of the real thing; of what living is like for God. If only God would reveal to us the truth about such matters and end this speculation! Surely that is not too much to ask?

But it seems that God relishes the mystery and likes to keep us in ignorance during our earthly lives. God only knows why, and I can only hope that despite all of the stresses and strains, God is ultimately merciful. I hope and pray that death marks a transition to a more peaceful place for all of us, and that somewhere out there heaven is a reality.

✣ 34 ✣

ALL IS TRANSPARENT AND
HARMONIOUS TO HIS EYE

16th January 2014

Today I stumbled upon a beautiful piece of writing by the 19th Century preacher Octavius Winslow. Despite not being a Christian myself, I feel a deep affinity with the view of God presented in the poem. It seems to fit in well with the theme of this blog – the 'perfect chaos' of God's world.

All is Transparent and Harmonious to His Eye!

(From Octavius Winslow's, "My Times in God's Hand")

We live in a world of mysteries.

They meet our eye, awaken our inquiry,

and baffle our investigation at every step.

Nature is a vast arcade of mysteries.

Science is a mystery.

Truth is a mystery.

Religion is a mystery.

Our existence is a mystery.

The future of our being is a mystery.

And God, who alone can explain all mysteries,

is the greatest mystery of all. How little do

we understand of the inexplicable wonders of a

wonder working God, "whose thoughts are a great

deep," and "whose ways are past finding out."

But to God nothing is mysterious.

In His purpose, nothing is unfixed.

In His forethought, nothing is unknown.

In His providence, nothing is contingent.

His glance pierces the future as vividly

as it beholds the past. "He knows the

end from the beginning."

All His doings are parts of a divine,

eternal, and harmonious plan.

He may make "darkness his secret place; His

pavilion round about him dark waters, and

thick clouds of the skies," and to human vision

His dispensations may appear gloomy, discrepant,

and confused. Yet He is "working all things

after the counsel of His own will," and all is

transparent and harmonious to His eye!

35

MORNING ANXIETY AND
DEPRESSION

26th February 2014

Most days I wake up around 8am with a strange and uncomfortable feeling in my body. It is a mixture of anxiety and depression, and it makes it really difficult to get out of bed. The feeling is always worse if I have a busy day of appointments ahead, but even when I have a clear day the feeling is still there. Most days I will lie in bed until after 10am, unable to shake off the feeling and begin the day with any sense of peace or excitement.

I remember this feeling from when I was working for Age Concern Oxfordshire in 2007. I was taking the antipsychotic Olanzapine, which makes you want to sleep for ages, making it particularly difficult to get up in the morning. I was working a 9-5 job as a busy administrator, and getting to work on time was a nightmare. I remember that during the walk to work each morning I would normally consider taking a detour to the doctor and getting signed off sick with depression, but I was determined to live a normal life so most days I would just push through and get to work by 9am.

In retrospect, I shouldn't have been working. The side effects of the Olanzapine were so severe that I was like a zombie for much of each morning. I felt depressed for the whole day, and working a busy job in those circumstances was just too much. But I felt a certain pressure from my father, with whom I was living, to keep on working. He wanted to see me live a normal working life and would have hated to have me mooching around the house all day feeling depressed. Whereas I really needed time and space to recover, he wanted me to push on through and carry on working.

At the moment, I am living in London in a shared house with other people with mental health difficulties. I honestly don't feel I can work with the crippling anxiety and depression that I wake up with each morning. Sometimes I think the feeling is linked to the antipsychotics I am taking (this time it's Depixol), sometimes I think it's the result of life circumstances weighing me down, and sometimes I think this feeling is just part of who I am, and always will be.

I am hoping to find some way to stop feeling this morning depression. I have a medical review coming up on 10th March and I'm going to talk everything through with my doctor. I would be prepared to try an anti-depressant if my doctor thinks that will solve the problem. Otherwise, it might help to try a reduction in the dose of the antipsychotic I am taking. Or perhaps I should try Cognitive Behavioural

Therapy again. Something has to change, as I have been feeling suicidal in recent weeks.

I have a diagnosis of schizoaffective disorder, and I have to accept that part of my illness is to experience spells of depression. This needs to be managed in the best way possible, but having this condition makes it very difficult to live a 'normal' life. I would love to be able to get up feeling a sense of energy and anticipation about the day ahead, but I find that nothing excites me or motivates me in a way that would counteract the anxiety and depression.

Having a couple of really good close friends is a massive help. Just knowing that I can express my feelings without fear or inhibition is a really big boost, and that's what gets me through the day most days. Without my friends I would be truly lost at the moment.

36

EXPLORING COGNITIVE BEHAVIOURAL THERAPY

16th March 2014

Earlier this week I had a medical review with my psychiatrist and care coordinator. I was quite nervous about the appointment; this was my first review in almost a year and it felt as though there was an awful lot (too much!) to talk about.

I have been really struggling with my mental health recently. Although I have no schizophrenic symptoms such as delusions and psychosis, my mood is very low at times and I have been having some suicidal thoughts. I wake up each morning with severe anxiety and depression, and I struggle with the onset of panic attacks perhaps once or twice a week.

After explaining all of this to my psychiatrist in the review meeting, he was quick to mention Cognitive Behavioural Therapy (CBT) and he described this as the first and most effective treatment he would recommend for my symptom profile. I explained that I was sceptical about attempting a talking therapy when my symptoms seemed so physical, but the only other option offered to me was anti-depressants, and I am even more sceptical about those!

I asked to be referred for CBT and was told the waiting list would be around 3 months, which doesn't seem too bad. I went to my local library and got out a book called 'Teach Yourself CBT' which I hoped would serve as a good introduction to the therapy.

Actually, this isn't my first experience of CBT. I attended a 10 week group CBT course run by Oxfordshire Mind a few years ago. I found that particular course largely unhelpful, but it did serve as a good introduction to the tools and methods of CBT.

As I have been reading the 'Teach Yourself CBT' book I have been using some of the methods from the book to challenge my negative thought patterns. For example, yesterday, when I felt the onset of a panic attack after going for a walk in a busy park, I lay on my bed and began to evaluate why I was feeling panicky, whether it was rational, and whether I should really be feeling more calm.

As I reasoned with myself I did feel the panic symptoms ease somewhat. This gives me confidence that the methods of CBT may actually help me with some of the difficult emotions I experience on a daily basis. I am feeling a little more positive now about attending a one-to-one CBT course at my local hospital. And to have a little hope, at a time like this, is a really good thing.

37

AUTOGENIC TRAINING

23rd March 2014

I recently rediscovered Autogenic Training, which is an effective technique for reducing stress and anxiety and the onset of panic attacks. It is a simple technique but works really well to restore the balance between the sympathetic and parasympathetic branches of the autonomic nervous system. If that sounds complicated, let's just say it's very relaxing!

If you feel like giving it a go, follow the instructions below.

Autogenic Training

As you lie quietly with your eyes closed, your legs straight, and your arms by your sides, repeat each of the following steps 5 times in your head, and after the fifth time use the affirmation, "I am completely calm". After each step move on to the next one and repeat the process. Work through the 6 steps in order and you should feel gradually more relaxed as the steps progress.

1. My right arm is heavy

2. My right arm is warm

3. My heart is beating calmly and regularly

4. My breathing is calm and regular

5. My abdomen is flowingly warm

6. My forehead is pleasantly cool

You can end the session with the affirmation "Tonight I will sleep deeply and peacefully" – repeat this five times as well, and then just rest in the peace of your body for a few minutes. Alternatively, if you have more time, you can repeat the process, going through the steps one by one a second time.

The more you practise this simple training, the more aware of your body you will be, and the easier you will find it to move through the steps. It should make you feel grounded, present, and relaxed.

❧ 38 ❧

LIFE AFTER DEATH

11th July 2014

I believe that consciousness is eternal. What I mean by this is that there never was or will be a time when you were/are not alive. Just because we don't remember being babies doesn't mean we weren't once babies, and in the same way, I believe we existed long before birth, but do not have a recollection of that time.

In order for you to understand why I believe this I need to say something about my conception of God. I believe God is all there is. All creatures and even material things are a part of God. God is omnipresent, so there is not one atom in the cosmos that is separate from God. An attribute of God's nature is existence. This being so, it is impossible for God to cease existing, even for a moment, in all eternity. Because we are all part of God, we share in that nature, and therefore exist eternally.

It is a mystery to me what exactly happens before birth and after death. God has not given me a revelation or insight into what happens. But I am quite sure there is a continuation of consciousness, and I believe we probably enter into another realm. The experience of waking up from life into death might be akin to waking up from a long dream into our present waking state.

I am curious about what we might be able to do in order to prepare ourselves for life after death. Not being a Christian or a person of any other particular faith, there are not any particular doctrines that I adhere to concerning the afterlife. There may well be a heaven-like realm, but how do we get there? If you are a Christian, then faith in Jesus is of course central. If you are a Muslim, then good works in accordance with the guidance of the Qur'an are of paramount importance. But if you do not adhere to a particular faith, how do you prepare for life after death?

To be honest, I don't know the answer to this question. I often pray to God asking Him to help me to use this life in order to prepare for the infinitely longer next one, but I am yet to receive a revelation of what I need to do. I have spent years exploring philosophy and spirituality, but the question remains unanswered.

I do have some reassurance, however. I believe that God is in control of all action in the cosmos, including all human action. So there is no free will. In a sense, this takes the pressure off, because I can have faith that God will unfold every aspect of my life in perfect accordance with His divine will.

So you could say it is ultimately up to God how I behave in this life, and how I prepare for the next life.

❧ 39 ❧

PRAY FOR A MIRACLE

28th September 2014

There is too much suffering in the world. There is the suffering that makes the headlines; conflict in Iraq and Syria or the Ebola virus for instance. Then there is the suffering that we don't read about in the newspapers; the homeless woman in central London or the young man with cancer. Every day there are countless people suffering in hospital, in psychiatric hospital, in prison, on the street, at work, and in their homes. So many people experience fear, pain, depression, anxiety, panic, hopelessness and despair. This is the agonising truth of life on earth.

And then there is the God, who I know is real, who is above all of these problems. The one true God of all creation has all the power in the universe, and could stop all of this terrible suffering in an instant if He so wished. I know that a breakthrough is possible. I know that God hears our prayers and so

I often pray for a miracle, whether it be the return of Jesus or something else, that will lead to peace and joy for all God's creatures on Earth. Do you believe that a breakthrough is possible?

It is hard to understand why God creates such suffering in our world. I have offered some possible explanations elsewhere on this blog and in my books. But it is clear to me that God is in control, and so I call on you my friends to say a prayer each day for a breakthrough – a miracle – that will bring peace to every creature on earth. Please, let us hope and pray. The stakes are too high not to give it a try. Thank you.

❧ IV ❧

2015

40

A RESPONSE TO 'STEPHEN FRY ON GOD'

8th February 2015

I recently watched a video clip that went viral in which Stephen Fry makes some very stark criticisms of God. In the clip, Fry is answering the question of what he would say to God if he came face to face with Him after death.

Fry responds by referencing the "theodicy" question, which simply put is "why would an all-powerful God permit (or create) suffering and evil?" Fry proceeds to give a couple of examples of terrible evils, before describing God as "utterly, utterly evil" and as "a capricious, mean-minded, stupid God, who creates a world which is so full of injustice and pain."

I can sympathise with Fry's views, and the theodicy question is one that I have spent a lot of time pondering. It certainly seems as though there is horrendous suffering in the world, and if God is all-powerful, which I firmly believe He is, why does He create such suffering?

My response to Fry's comments takes a bit of explaining, but bare with me and please consider seriously what I have to say. I believe that in order to answer the theodicy question we need to look to God's own nature, and the way in which God may Himself suffer.

I believe there are two important ways in which God could be said to suffer. Firstly, I believe God is omnipresent. This means God is all that exists. We can expand on this and say, in ultimate terms, God is totally alone. I realise the world contains apparently separate beings, but if God is alone and omnipresent, then we are all expressions of God, controlled and guided by God. Life is like a puppet show, with God in control. I would argue that God creates such a diversity of creatures, including human beings with all our various beliefs and ways of life, because being supremely alone is a kind of suffering and created beings are as close as God can get to experiencing relationship. Might it be true that God experiences a hellish loneliness?

There is another way in which God could be said to suffer. An aspect of God's nature is existence. This is an existence which is eternal; without beginning or end. God is necessarily alive. For God, there is never an ending. There is no option of suicide. There is no chance to 'switch off'. God must live endlessly even if He doesn't want to. What must that be like? Isn't that a kind of hell?

So we can see that there are several ways in which God might experience hellish suffering or agony. In light of this, we might

better understand why God creates such suffering in His creatures. Perhaps God wants to give us a taste of "the real thing";
of what ultimate reality is like for Him. If God experiences
both good and evil as aspects of His own being, then why
shouldn't He give us a taste of all this as part of our own lives
and deaths?

I'm aware that this view is one that is not compatible with the
core beliefs of the Abrahamic religions (Christianity, Islam,
and Judaism), because, unlike those religions, I believe God is
in control and therefore that we don't have free will.

✺ 41 ✺

SUFFERING, DEATH, AND THE AFTERLIFE

12th February 2015

When I was a Christian I had great faith that there would be a place in heaven waiting for me when I died. This faith gave me the confidence to live more freely and fearlessly. There are many things I miss about being a Christian, and this confidence in a blissful afterlife is one of them.

The reason I couldn't continue being a Christian is because I found deep flaws in the theology of the church (explained in detail in my book *Ultimate Truth: God Beyond Religion*). I don't believe in free will. Instead, I believe God is actively in control of everything that happens in the universe. This means ideas like sin, judgement, and the devil, make no sense to me. These are deeply significant ideas and problems that I could not overcome, even after lengthy discussions with Christian friends and pastors and priests. I simply had to leave the faith and live with my new understanding.

Since I have turned away from Christianity, the problem of death has become a little more complex. These days, despite extensive exploration of different faith groups, I do not associate myself with any particular religion. So there are no scriptures to comfort me and no pastors to tell me how to live in order to achieve that great prize of Christian faith – a place in heaven.

I know there is a God and I believe there will be an afterlife for everyone, regardless of their beliefs. I believe this because my intuition tells me consciousness, by it's very nature, is eternal. It is impossible to not exist. There has never been a time when I haven't existed, and there will never be an ending to my existence. Instead, there are simply transitions into different states. I believe this because we are all expressions of God, and part of God's nature is existence. It is impossible for God (and therefore us) to stop existing.

Living for eternity seems appealing but what really frightens me is suffering. I am frightened of suffering whether it be in this life or during the event of death or in the afterlife. Believing as I do that God is in control of all, I am constantly and fervently praying and reaching out to God as I desperately don't want to suffer hellish experiences. Through my spiritual journey and mental illness I have had a small taste of suffering, and I know how much worse things could be. I even believe hell is possible.

But having said all this I still have a good amount of hope. I believe that God is ultimately merciful and although He might give us a terrible taste of suffering, that suffering is always under control, and limited. Unlike many Christians,

Muslims, and Jews, I believe that God is in control of all our suffering, and I explain why God might cause us to suffer elsewhere on this blog and in more depth in my books.

Death is to be feared, as the unknown is always frightening. But most fearful of all is suffering, as we live under the control of an infinitely powerful God who could drag us through hell if He so chose. I suggest that we all need to pray fervently to God for mercy, and to try to come to a deeper understanding of why it is that God causes us to suffer.

42

A RESPONSE TO RICHARD DAWKINS ON THE ABSURDITY OF THE CRUCIFIXION

15th February 2015

There's a lot that I don't agree with Richard Dawkins about. But he once said this in an interview:

> *"It's a horrible idea that God, this paragon of wisdom and knowledge and power, couldn't think of a better way to forgive us our sins than to come down to Earth in his alter ego as his son and have himself hideously tortured and executed so that he could forgive himself."*

This strikes a chord with me and seems to encapsulate something rather absurd about the Christian faith. I think the central point here is one that I discuss often in my books and on this blog – the problem of free will. Christians might argue that in the act of Jesus' crucifixion God is not forgiving *himself* but sinful human beings.

When Dawkins talks about God 'forgiving himself', the implication is that God is in control of sin and therefore that we don't have free will, which is also what I believe. If we don't have free will then the whole notion of forgiveness is absurd, because human beings can have done nothing freely that would need forgiving. In this light, the story of the crucifixion is very strange indeed.

The reason why I don't believe we have free will is because I believe in a God who is omnipotent, omniscient, and omnipresent. Everything that exists is a part of God, and this means that God must be in control of everything that happens, including what is referred to as 'sin'.

The following quote from Epicurus is apposite here:

> Is God willing to prevent evil, but not able?
> Then he is not omnipotent.
> Is he able, but not willing?
> Then he is malevolent.
> Is he both able, and willing?
> Then whence cometh evil?
> Is he neither able nor willing?
> Then why call him God.

My response to Epicurus would be that God is able to prevent evil, but not willing. But I disagree that this necessarily makes God malevolent. It may be that God has very good reasons for creating evil in the world. Perhaps, if God himself suffers terribly, then He creates evil to give us a taste of what ultimate reality is like for Him − a perspective which I have explored in recent posts.

In summary, then, Richard Dawkins has highlighted that if God is in control of our existence (as I believe He is), the story of human redemption through Jesus' crucifixion makes very little sense.

43

A PRAYER OF THANKS

14th June 2015

Today, Almighty Father, I give you thanks.

When I was an unbeliever,

you were shaping and moulding my character;

working out a plan for my life with great care and intricacy.

You sent teachers to help me through struggles

and to develop my curious mind.

Lord, I was lost in a wilderness for so many years,

and you used my trials to bring me closer to you.

I now know that you were holding me and protecting me in my darkest moments.

Your light was there, out of sight, but you were watching over me.

You gave me a taste of depression and despair,

of pain and suffering,

but you led me through those darkest hours to a place of greater peace.

Knowing you, Lord, has been my life's great blessing.

I praise you for the light you have poured into my suffering soul

and for the precious freedoms you have afforded me.

You are there when I pray, Lord, listening and guiding.

You are also there when I am lost and confused.

You have blessed me so richly and saved me from countless hostilities.

I love you, Lord, with my whole heart, soul, mind, and strength, and I pray that you would keep me in your peace forever.

Amen.

✵ 44 ✵

WHAT IS THE MEANING OF LIFE?

18th June 2015

I have been an atheist, a new age spiritualist and a Christian, and I've been drawn to different teachings and philosophies from around the world at different times in my life. I spent a good deal of my adult life searching painfully and desperately for Truth.

My life has taken on a different meaning since I became aware that there really is a God. When God reveals himself to you, it changes everything. It is both wonderful and frightening. The God that I now know is all-powerful and has created our universe and everything in it. God is in control of the perfect chaos of existence on Earth and throughout the universe. All of the good, and all of the bad, are the result of God acting in creation.

When I was a Christian, my life was filled with purpose. I was on a mission to discover more about Jesus by studying the Bible and I was very evangelical. Bringing people into the Christian faith was my ambition and this gave my life so much meaning. I thought that I would be a Christian for the rest of my life.

But things changed when I began to think in depth about some of the key teachings of Christianity. These teachings conflicted with my knowledge about God in a way that made me feel deeply uncomfortable. For instance, I know that a part of God's nature is that he is omnipresent (everywhere) and therefore *all is God*. There cannot be free will – *all will is God's will*.

If all will is God's will then it is not coherent to talk of sin, or the fall of man, or punishment in hell, or the devil. Knowing that there is no free will means I can no longer call myself a Christian. I now know that the whole of existence is contained within God, and wherever there is action in existence God is the animating force.

The meaning of life, I have come to understand, is that we are all part of a cosmic game with God in control. God needs to stay entertained and occupied for all eternity, so he has created this complex universe in order to express many different aspects of himself and of reality.

❧ 45 ❧

THE DEVIL DOESN'T EXIST

1st August 2015

The Bible is full of references to the devil (also called Satan, Beelzebul, the enemy, the evil one, etc). It would be fair to say that the existence of this being is central to the Christian faith. We learn from the gospels that Jesus, when carrying out His ministry and His miracles, was often casting out demons and rebuking the devil.

But who or what exactly is the devil? There are plenty of scriptures that mention the devil in many different contexts. In one scripture he is referred to as a "great dragon" and an "ancient serpent" (Revelation 12:9). Elsewhere he is described as "the ruler of this world" (John 12:32). In another scripture the devil is described as the "son of Dawn" who has "fallen from heaven" (Isaiah 14:12).

The impression that one gets when reading the scriptures that mention the devil is that he is in opposition to God, and does not serve God. Instead, he is the lord of temptation and betrayal. He tempts Jesus in the wilderness (Luke 4:1-2), and betrays Jesus through the actions of Judas Iscariot (John 13:2). Many Christians argue that while God is perfectly good, the devil is responsible for all evil in the world.

But let us consider whether it is really possible for any being to exist in opposition to God. I believe that God created this universe and everything in it. Theologians will tell you about attributes of God such as omnipotence, omniscience, and omnipresence. In other words, God is all-powerful, all-knowing, and everywhere. If this is true, it means that everything that happens, and everything that has ever happened, is and always has been under the direct control of God.

In this context, is a rebellion against God by the devil really possible? If God is omnipresent, that means that nothing else exists apart from God. The whole of existence is part of God, and God is in control of everything. One would have to conclude that either the devil doesn't exist, or he exists but is under God's control. But why would a benevolent God create and control a being whose purpose is death, destruction, and torment?

Some Christians might respond that the devil fell from grace and acts of his own free will, as do his earthly followers. But this argument fails. It fails because, as we have said, omnipresence is part of God's nature. If this is true, there can be no free will. All of existence is created and sustained by

God. He is all-powerful and in control of everything that happens.

I believe, therefore, that it is wise to see sin and shame and death and destruction as under the direct control of God. After all, isn't that why we pray to Him? Isn't that why we reach out to Him? Don't we know, deep in our hearts, that God has all power, is in control, and is the solution to every problem?

Perhaps God has created an evil spiritual being, a devil, in opposition to Himself as part of the game of life. Perhaps the devil is part of a grand scheme to make existence more interesting for God, and to express different facets of His power and His nature. But if this is the case, I would still have to conclude that the devil doesn't really exist, because he is a part of God and is under God's control. There is no escaping the Ultimate Truth, which is that as an independent being with free will, the devil doesn't really exist.

46

WHY I AM GETTING BAPTISED

1st September 2015

Friends, it may come as a surprise to you that I am going to get baptised. I say this because if you have read some of my blog posts, you will know that I have had a lot of intellectual problems with Christianity over the last few years.

Even through my struggles with Christianity, I have always believed in God. I have been going to Westminster Cathedral once or twice a week to pray for several years, but I haven't felt comfortable attending Mass because there were aspects of the liturgy that I found puzzling and nonsensical. For instance, I had problems with the idea of original sin and I couldn't believe that we have free will. I should add that this never stopped me having a deep awe for God and for Jesus. But I didn't feel I could become a committed Christian.

When I was living in Wandsworth Town last year, there was a small group of Christians from a local church who used to congregate by the shopping centre every week on a Saturday for 'outreach'. They would sing songs about Jesus and hand out leaflets encouraging people to explore the Christian faith. I used to chat with them, buy them the occasional coffee, and share with them the struggles that I was having with Christianity. And I asked them to pray for me.

I know that other friends and family have been praying for me too. I have been to several churches in the past and met some wonderful friends who have kept me in their prayers even while I was blogging about why I couldn't bring myself to commit to Christianity. Despite all these prayers, I began to think of myself as a 'post-Christian' thinker, and had an ongoing struggle in my spirit regarding the role of Jesus in my life.

In recent weeks, I have been reading the Bible every day, and watching sermons by amazing Christian speakers like Nicky Gumbel and Bishop T.D. Jakes online. All the while, I felt the strong pull of faith, but also the intellectual resistance to some of what these preachers were saying. I was beginning to think I would have to live with this struggle for the rest of my life.

But something amazing happened on the 27th August. I had been reading the Bible and was sitting quietly in bed ready to switch off the light and go to sleep. I was suddenly overtaken by a strong conviction and these words sprang into my mind: 'You are going to get baptised'. I felt shock, but it was also an amazing feeling and I knew these words were coming from

God. Before I could recover, another conviction came to my mind: 'You are then going to take Holy Communion'. I was overcome with a feeling of great peace and joy. I stayed awake all night in excitement and prayer, and I felt overjoyed by these revelations.

Since that night the conviction that I am going to get baptised and take Holy Communion hasn't left me. In fact, God has been setting the wheels in motion and all the preparations for my baptism are in place. I am getting baptised this Sunday, 6th September, in the Baptist church from where the outreach team that I met outside the shopping centre came.

Despite all of my struggles with Christianity, I know that Jesus shed his blood for me, and for all of us. I know that the crucifixion was an atoning sacrifice and a declaration of God's love and forgiveness for humanity. I know from my Bible studies that there is so much more to existence than this short earthly life, and it's important to live with eternity in mind.

I believe baptism is a sacrament from God, allowing people to be cleansed of their sins and to share in the death and resurrection of Jesus. I'm aware that baptism marks a commitment to the Christian faith, and I feel that I am being called to put aside my intellectual difficulties with Christianity and step into a new phase of my life living by faith in Jesus.

If you are a believer, please pray for me that my faith remains strong and my baptism goes well on Sunday.

❧ 47 ❧

UNDERSTANDING THE DEVIL

5th September 2015

Today I was reading from the book of Matthew and I came across a passage that has influenced my understanding of what exactly the devil is. I have had problems understanding the devil as a being in competition with God, because I believe God has all power in existence, and therefore how could a being like the devil exist in opposition to Him?

The passage that inspired me was Matthew 16:21-23, which says this:

> *From that time on Jesus began to explain to his disciples that he must go to Jerusalem and suffer many things at the hands of the elders, the chief priests and the teachers of the law, and that he must be killed and on the third day be raised to life. Peter took him aside and began to rebuke him. "Never, Lord!"*

he said. "This shall never happen to you!" Jesus turned and
said to Peter, "Get behind me, Satan! You are a stumbling
block to me; you do not have in mind the concerns of God, but
merely human concerns."

When he rebukes Peter, it is clear to me that Jesus doesn't consider him to *literally* be Satan (after all, he is one of Jesus' chosen disciples), but instead he is speaking about Satan in a *metaphorical* way. The devil in this instance is a spirit of distrust and a lack of faith.

We all experience distrust, but does this mean we have Satan inside of us too? I would argue that this is only the case if we understand Satan to be a certain spirit or attitude, rather than that fallen angel with the red horns as he is often depicted.

It is also true that in the Bible people are given demonic possession by God in order that He might be glorified through their healing by Jesus. Again, the devils in question aren't horned beasts or fiery dragons, but are spirits that come from God to serve a specific purpose. There is a theme in the New Testament that God gives people ailments in order that He might be glorified by Jesus' miraculous healing ministry. See, for example, John 9:2-3:

His disciples asked him, "Rabbi, who sinned, this man or his
parents, that he was born blind?" "Neither this man nor his
parents sinned," said Jesus, "but this happened so that the
works of God might be displayed in him."

Here we see that the ailments of the sick are given to them by God (and I believe we can include demonic possession) according to His higher purposes. When viewed in this light, I find it much easier to accept Biblical references to the devil or Satan, as He is not some kind of great dragon that is literally fighting with God, but is a spirit under God's control.

❧ 48 ❧

MY BAPTISM TODAY

6th September 2015

This morning I awoke to clear blue sky – it was a truly beautiful sight. I knew that today was the day I would be sealing my discipleship of Jesus Christ, and having my sins symbolically washed clean via the sacrament of baptism. I was of course nervous, but engulfing that anxiety was a sense of peace and a trust in God.

When I got to the church, my father was waiting on the steps by the entrance. We embraced and he told me he had had an amazingly smooth journey to London. Praise God! Looking up to the sunshiny sky we shared that famous scripture together: "This is the day that the Lord has made; We will rejoice and be glad in it." (Psalm 118:24).

My father was baptised as a child. My mother, who passed away in 2003, was an atheist. My parents made the decision that they wouldn't baptise my sister and I as children; they would let us grow up and decide for ourselves whether or not to become Christians. I respect that decision that my parents made.

The church service today was so wonderful. The worship songs were glorious, the sermon was inspiring, my baptism was beautiful, and the Holy Communion was such a blessing. The scripture that was the focus of the service was this: "I am not ashamed of the Gospel, for it is the power of God that brings salvation to everyone who believes." (Romans 1:16).

I have a long way to go on my journey to understand the Word of God and to live in the way that Jesus instructed. But I trust in the power of the Holy Spirit to guide me day by day, and little by little, to reveal God's truth to me. I am anticipating that I may have struggles at times, but my prayer is that I will not stray from Biblical teaching and will continue to be inspired by the Gospel.

Just before my baptism, I read out a prayer to the church that I wrote when I woke up this morning. I would like to share it with you, in the hope that it encourages you and blesses you:

Today, Almighty Father, I give you thanks.

Thank you for the gospel, Lord, which is salvation unto all who believe.

Thank you Lord for restoring my faith in your beloved Son, in whom you are well pleased.

Thank you Lord, that though I am a wretched sinner, your wrath does not burn against me, but instead Lord you have made a way to salvation by the blood of the lamb.

Today Lord I beg you for mercy and ask that you would cleanse me of my sins in the blessed name of Jesus.

Please bless this church Lord and all who are gathered here today in your name.

We love you, Heavenly Father, and may all honour and glory be yours forever and ever.

Amen.

This is just a short blog post, but in truth, I could write a book about today. So many happy memories to cherish for the rest of my life. In fact, I think this was the best day of my life. Glory to God in Highest Heaven!

49

HE'S JUST A PRAYER AWAY

8th September 2015

If you've never been to Westminster Cathedral in London, I would highly recommend a visit. It's a beautiful building, filled with the presence of God. And it's very peaceful, so a great place to pray.

Last year I visited the cathedral with a friend, who went into the cathedral shop and bought me a small gift. The gift was a little card with a poem on it. It's a simple and beautiful poem, and today I'd like to share it with you for your encouragement.

Here's the poem:

> *No matter what your troubles are*
> *no difference large or small*
> *each upset that may come your way*

each time you slightly fall
The smallest fear you've ever had
is always known by God
each step you've walked he's counted
on every road you've trod
So never feel that you're alone
when shadows cloud your day
but speak His name and you will see
He's just a prayer away.

50

A FEW WORDS ABOUT JESUS

22nd September 2015

The Bible says He's the King of the Jews, He's the King of Israel, He's the King of righteousness, He's the King of the ages, He's the King of heaven, He's the King of glory, He's the King of Kings and He is the Lord of Lords.

David says the Heavens declare the glory of God and the firmament shows us His handiwork; no means of measure can define His limitless love. No far-seeing telescope can bring into visibility the coastline of his shoreless supply. No barriers can hinder Him from pouring out His blessing. He's enduringly strong, He's entirely sincere, He's eternally steadfast, He's immortally graceful, He's imperially powerful, He's impartially merciful.

He's God's Son, He's the sinners' Saviour, He's the centrepiece of civilisation, He stands alone in Himself, He's august, He's unique, He's unparalleled, He's unprecedented, He's supreme, He's pre-eminent, He's the loftiest idea in literature, He's the highest personality in philosophy, He's the supreme problem in higher criticism, He's the fundamental doctrine of true theology, He's the cardinal necessity of spiritual religion.

He's the miracle of the age, He's the only one able to supply all of our needs simultaneously, He gives strength to the weak, He's available for the tempted and the tired, He sympathises and He saves, He guards and He guides, He heals the sick, He cleansed the lepers, He forgives sinners, He discharges debtors, He delivers the captives, He defends the feeble, He blesses the young, He serves the unfortunate, He regards the aged, He rewards the diligent, and He beautifies the meek.

He's the key of knowledge, He's the wellspring of wisdom, He's the doorway of deliverance, He's the pathway of peace, He's the roadway of righteousness, He's the highway of holiness, He's the gateway of glory, He's the master of the mighty, He's the captain of the conquerors, He's the head of the heroes, He's the leader of the legislators, He's the overseer of the overcomers, He's the governor of governors, He's the prince of princes, He's the King of Kings and He's the Lord of Lords.

His office is manifold, His promise is sure, His life is matchless, His goodness is limitless, His mercy is everlasting, His love never changes, His word is enough, His grace is sufficient, His reign is righteous, His yoke is easy, and His burden is light.

I wish I could describe Him to you!

He's indescribable, He's incomprehensible, He's invincible, He's irresistible, the heaven of heavens cannot contain Him, let alone a man explain Him, you can't get Him out of your mind, you can't outlive Him and you can't live without Him, the pharisees couldn't stand Him, when they found out they couldn't stop Him, Pilate couldn't find any fault in Him, Herod couldn't kill Him, Death couldn't handle Him, and the grave couldn't hold Him.

He always has been, and He always will be, He had no predecessor, and He'll have no successor, there was nobody before Him and there'll be nobody after Him, you can't impeach Him and He's not going to resign.

The glory is all His!

"For thine is the kingdom and the power and the glory, forever and ever, Amen."

❦ 51 ❦

THE IMPORTANCE OF PRAYER

3rd October 2015

One of my favourite scriptures is Philippians 4:6-7, which reads,

> *Be anxious for nothing, but in everything by prayer and supplication, with thanksgiving, let your requests be made known to God; and the peace of God, which surpasses all understanding, will guard your hearts and minds through Christ Jesus.*

The above scripture, written by Paul in his letter to the Philippians in the New Testament, tells us a lot about how and why to pray. The word 'supplication' means "the action of asking or begging for something earnestly or humbly". So when we pray, Paul says we should be honest and humble. We should acknowledge the greatness of God, and recognise that as we pray He already knows everything that is going on in our hearts and in our lives; we don't need to disguise the truth.

I heard an interesting message from the Holy Trinity Brompton vicar Nicky Gumbel recently in which he suggested there are three important components to prayer. He said we should be childlike in our prayers by remembering to say 'please, sorry, and thank you'. If you're not used to praying, this is an excellent way to start. You might say please in relation to your needs, sorry in relation to your sins, and thank you in relation to your gifts and blessings.

Today I was doing outreach with my church, which is where we go out onto the streets to chat to people about the gospel and about God. I met a lovely man who spoke to me about how certain events in his life had caused him to distance himself from God. He was carrying a certain amount of regret and even guilt about a situation in his life which took place many years ago. I felt prompted to pray for him, and I explained that it was precisely for situations such as his that Jesus came and died; allowing us all to be in right relationship with God if only we would have faith and ask God for forgiveness.

When I prayed for this man, I asked for God's blessing and favour to be upon his life, and I know that God heard my prayer. I felt a real sense of God's presence while I prayed, and I trust that God will begin to untie the knots in this man's heart, and bring him back into right relationship with Jesus.

Jesus teaches us about how to pray. You will no doubt be familiar with The Lord's Prayer, which can be found in the Bible in Matthew 6:9-13. This prayer varies slightly according to different translations but the version I pray (which I remember for my school days) goes like this:

Our Father in heaven,
Hallowed be thy name.
Thy kingdom come,
Thy will be done,
On earth, as it is in heaven.
Give us this day our daily bread,
And forgive us our trespasses,
As we forgive those who trespass against us.
And lead us not into temptation,
But deliver us from evil.
For thine is the kingdom, the power, and the glory,
Forever and ever. Amen.

God doesn't always answer prayer in the way we expect. But the very act of praying is an act of humility. And when we humble ourselves before God, acknowledging Him in all His greatness, power, and glory, He never fails to respond and to speak into our hearts and into our lives. He is working all things together for good for those who love Him and are called according to His purpose (Romans 8:28).

Perhaps you have never said a prayer. Or perhaps you haven't prayed for a long time. Perhaps you are not even sure whether there is a God, and so the idea of praying seems strange and foreign. I would urge you to humble yourself today, and take a

leap of faith, and reach out to God in prayer. The treasure −
and I mean spiritual treasure, not earthly treasure − of our
Lord Jesus Christ is waiting.

EVIDENCE FOR JESUS' DIVINITY

5th October 2015

In the New Testament there are many instances which reveal that Jesus had the supernatural ability to know others completely even when meeting them for the first time. I believe this is a really important aspect of Jesus' divine nature because only God has that kind of knowledge. If Jesus were merely a prophet, and not the messiah, he would not have this ability.

Here are a few of the scriptures that reveal this quality in Jesus:

John 1:42: "And he brought him to Jesus. And when Jesus beheld him, he said, Thou art Simon the son of Jona: thou shalt be called Cephas, which is by interpretation, A stone."

John 1:47: "Jesus saw Nathanael coming to him, and saith of him, Behold an Israelite indeed, in whom is no guile!"

John 4:29 (The Woman at the Well): "Come, see a man, which told me all things that ever I did: is not this the Christ?"

John 6:61: "When Jesus knew in himself that his disciples murmured at it, he said unto them, Doth this offend you?"

John 6:64: "But there are some of you that believe not. For Jesus knew from the beginning who they were that believed not, and who should betray him."

It is fascinating to explore what exactly it is about Jesus that makes Him unique. In a blog post which I wrote several years ago, I suggested that Jesus was very human but not divine in any unique way. I wrote that aspects of Jesus' life, death, and resurrection were miraculous, but that there are many other figures in Scripture through whom God worked similar miracles.

But this supernatural attribute of knowing everything about a person is unique to the Son of God, Jesus Christ. I believe this sets Jesus apart from the other prophets, and demonstrates His divinity; Jesus is fully God and fully human.

❧ 53 ❧

BY HIS STRIPES WE ARE HEALED

10th October 2015

O Lord of power and glory,

Have mercy on my soul!

You are the God of covenants,

Who promises salvation for your people.

In days of old, Lord,

You gave the law to your servant Moses,

You carved your commandments

On tablets of stone.

Your chosen people Israel

Were richly blessed by your mercy,

And your favour was upon them

As you saved them from their oppressors.

But your servants disgraced you, Lord,

By bowing down to idols

And worshiping foreign gods.

There were many times, Lord,

When your anger burned against your people

And you would not forgive them

For their transgressions.

But Lord, God of mercy,

You are kind and patient,

You are jealous, Lord,

But also forgiving!

You gave your people a second chance,

And a third chance,

You did not hold their sins against them.

For the world has been full of sin,

Since your servant Adam,

Disobeyed you in the Garden of Eden,

And ate the forbidden fruit.

You created us in your image, Lord,

But we are weak and sinful, unlike you.

We turn away from you, Lord,

Out of pride and selfishness.

We do not obey your commandments, Lord,

And we forget your truths,

We stray from the righteous path,

And many troubles befall us.

How would you deal with us, Lord,

Frail wretches that we are?

Will you ever find a way to forgive us?

Behold! The Lamb of God

Who takes away the sins of the world!

Jesus Christ is His name!

While we were still slaves to sin,

You sent your one and only Son,

To be born of a virgin,

And to live a blameless life,

To teach us about the truth,

And to help us find salvation.

Rejoice! For Jesus brings Good News,

A new and eternal covenant

For the forgiveness of sins;

A way that we can be right with God.

Your Son suffered agony on my behalf, Lord;

"He was wounded for our transgressions,

He was bruised for our iniquities:

The chastisement of our peace was upon him;

And by his stripes, we are healed."

Hallelujah! Lord, you have made a way,

You have brought hope to sinners,

And healing to the broken,

You have brought salvation to all who believe!

In my own life, Lord, I have greatly sinned,

And am worthy of your wrath.

But your Son is my redemption,

And I believe in Him!

Surely, Lord, I am forgiven,

And am blameless in your sight,

Because of the atoning sacrifice of your Son.

Lord, all things are possible with you.

You lift up who you will,

And you bring down who you will.

But as for me, Lord,

I will trust in the Gospel you have revealed to me,

And I will hope in you all day long!

Though my body is broken, Lord,

Yet will I trust in you.

Though death knocks at my door, Lord,

I will fear no evil;

"For thy rod and thy staff, they comfort me."

I will anoint myself with oil, Lord,

Trusting in your healing power.

I will read your Word each day, Lord,

And find comfort in your promises.

I will sing to you spiritual songs, Lord,

To thank you for your mercies.

Glory to you forever, Almighty Father!

Praise to the Lamb of God!

Make me whole again, Lord!

In the precious name of Jesus.

Amen.

❧ 54 ❧

FAITH THROUGH SUFFERING

8th November 2015

It's difficult to see loved ones from church suffering with serious health conditions. But it's such a relief to know that despite all they are going through, God loves them, and has a place for them with Jesus in heaven.

In the meantime, during this earthly existence, we have to have faith. We must be prayerful and find encouragement in God's Word. His ways are so far above our understanding, but the Bible gives us some wonderful truths to hang onto in our hour of need.

Here are a few scriptures that give me encouragement when I am suffering, or when I see others suffering:

"These things I have spoken to you, that in Me you may have

peace. In the world you will have tribulation; but be of good cheer, I have overcome the world." (John 16:33)

"Now may the God of hope fill you with all joy and peace in believing, that you may abound in hope by the power of the Holy Spirit." (Romans 15:13)

"Trust in the Lord with all your heart, and lean not on your own understanding; In all your ways acknowledge Him, and He shall direct your paths." (Proverbs 3:5-6)

As the saying goes, "If you're going through hell, keep going". And as the song goes, "Keep on keeping on". This lifetime is but a moment in eternity; let's not forget the spiritual riches that await us if we hold fast to our faith and live for the gospel of Christ, despite our adversity.

✺ 55 ✺

DEEP FELLOWSHIP

29th November 2015

Sometimes church is uplifting, sometimes inspiring, and sometimes challenging. Today brought a mixture of all three. We sang some of my favourite songs, including kicking off the service with 'O Come All Ye Faithful' to mark the start of advent. We also sang that classic hymn 'How Great Thou Art', and I couldn't help but sing my lungs out until my voice started croaking.

The more challenging part of the service came in the message delivered today by pastor Michael. Michael was speaking about fellowship in the church, and the focus of the message was 'deep fellowship', an idea which took a bit of explaining. The scripture that was the focus of the message was Ecclesiastes 4:9-12, which says this:

Two are better than one,

Because they have a good reward for their labor.
For if they fall, one will lift up his companion.
But woe to him who is alone when he falls,
For he has no one to help him up.
Again, if two lie down together, they will keep warm;
But how can one be warm alone?
Though one may be overpowered by another, two can with-
stand him.
And a threefold cord is not quickly broken.

These verses from Ecclesiastes talk of warmth, help, and reward, as examples of some of the benefits we find in having a true friend to help us in life.

In the context of church life, we need people who we can share with on a deep level. We need people who we can connect with in a meaningful way and not just talk about the superficial stuff. Part of church life should be forging relationships that allow us to share not only the easy parts of our testimonies, but those parts which we keep hidden for fear of the judgment or perhaps disdain of others.

I think that so many of us have secrets that we feel we can't talk about because we feel embarrassed or ashamed. And I count myself among that number. There are some things that I feel I want to share, but they are deeply personal, and to be perfectly honest, I'm afraid of how others would react if they heard what I had to say.

James 5:16 reads as follows: "Therefore confess your sins to each other and pray for each other so that you may be healed." There is an indication here that confession is a powerful tool that enables God to heal us, and I suppose this is a major function of the deep fellowship that our pastor was talking about today.

It takes time to build this kind of fellowship. I have only been attending my church for three months, and although I've met many wonderful people and made some great friends, there's no one that I feel I can share my deepest secrets with at this time. But it is partly about commitment and effort, and I will be praying that in time God will enable me to forge those bonds, even if it's just with one person, that will allow me to pour my heart out to a receptive and loving ear.

Of course, God knows us with a deep intimacy ("And even the very hairs on your head are numbered" Matthew 10:30) and it is perhaps easier to share things with Him, because we know that He is already aware of our deepest secrets. But in the realm of interpersonal dialogue, we need to nurture a deep level of fellowship and love our neighbour (Mark 12:31) enough for a profound trust to develop.

I was grateful for the challenge that pastor Michael blessed us with today. It has focused my prayers around the matter of deep fellowship, and in the coming months I will endeavour to grow closer to people in church so that we can share secrets and confess our sins together. "For all have sinned and fall short of the glory of God" (Romans 3:23). Perhaps, if we can share in this way, we might experience the love of God in a way that we hadn't previously thought possible.

❧ V ❧

2016

THE BIBLE AND PATIENCE

10th January 2016

I have encountered a variety of situations in my life recently which have really tested my patience. Sometimes it is little things that frustrate me, such as people throwing litter onto the street or when people stand at a crossing for ages and don't press the button, seemingly not realising that the lights won't change unless they do...

These are petty frustrations, but I have also been experiencing more serious frustrations. People driving recklessly, for instance. On several occasions recently I've seen cars drive straight through a red light in a busy area. And in a similar way, it frustrates me when cars stop right in the middle of a crossing, ignoring their duty to 'Keep Clear' of certain areas. Where is the common decency?

I have also been frustrated by people acting unprofessionally when they have a duty to be caring. I was in A&E recently and a security guard was flirting with two nurses for around 15 minutes when they all should have been working (they were definitely not on a break!). In another scenario, there's a parking attendant at one of my local supermarkets who is constantly on the phone and smoking cigarettes during work time. I don't want to be judgmental but it seems very thoughtless and unprofessional.

I should point out that I'm aware of how blessed I am in my life and I know there are countless people living with a much deeper level of frustration than I experience. I'm aware that we all have grumbles like those I have mentioned here in our lives. We all have to associate with people who we don't get along with all the time. And perhaps there are things that I do, even unconsciously, that frustrate others. I know I'm not perfect.

So what are we to do when we're feeling angry about life's frustrations? We should surely turn to the Holy Bible for guidance, for this is the Word of God, and as we read in 2 Timothy 3:16,

> *"All scripture is God-breathed and is useful for teaching, rebuking, correcting and training in righteousness"*

And what does the Bible say about patience? Here are some scriptures that are relevant:

> *"Rejoice in hope, be patient in tribulation, be constant in prayer."* (Romans 12:12)

"And let us not grow weary of doing good, for in due season we will reap, if we do not give up." (Galatians 6:9)

"Be not quick in your spirit to become angry, for anger lodges in the bosom of fools." (Ecclesiastes 7:9)

"Love is patient and kind; love does not envy or boast; it is not arrogant" (1 Corinthians 13:4)

"Know this, my beloved brothers: let every person be quick to hear, slow to speak, slow to anger" (James 1:19)

And here's a scripture that I find particularly helpful:

"Be still before the Lord and wait patiently for him; fret not yourself over the one who prospers in his way, over the man who carries out evil devices! Refrain from anger, and forsake wrath! Fret not yourself; it tends only to evil. For the evildoers shall be cut off, but those who wait for the Lord shall inherit the land." (Psalm 37:7-9)

I think one of the secrets to being patient is to keep our minds focused on our Heavenly Father and on spiritual things and not earthly things. We should always act in a way that makes us feel as though we are behaving righteously in the sight of God. We should live to please God and not to please others. Even if others frustrate us by their actions, we should lead by example. As Jesus famously said - *"Thou shalt love thy neighbour as thyself"* (Mark 12:31). And Jesus also taught us to love our enemies (Matthew 5:44).

So the next time you're feeling angry and as though your patience has run out, remember that God, through His Word, has taught us a great deal about how to handle these difficult emotions. My prayer is that as I continue to follow Jesus, God will shape me and teach me to be a more perfect and patient servant.

☙ 57 ❧

THE ROLE OF WOMEN IN CHURCH

31st January 2016

I'm currently attending a weekly prayer and Bible study group. The group is led by two women, Sarah and Heather. The session lasts for about an hour, and we sing traditional hymns, pray, and listen to Sarah and Heather speaking about Jesus and the Bible.

At the end of one session, a couple of weeks ago, I got chatting to a man who was sitting next to me. He strongly believes that women should not be leaders in the church, and is confident that this is what the Bible teaches.

I know that in the Anglican church there is an ongoing debate about the role of women and I was wondering whether the situation is as black and white as the man from the Bible study group was implying. So I did a little research, and I think the following points are key:

1) None of the apostles were women. However, we read in Luke that there were some women who supported Jesus and the apostles in their work:

> *Soon afterward he went on through cities and villages, proclaiming and bringing the good news of the kingdom of God. And the twelve were with him, [2] and also some women who had been healed of evil spirits and infirmities: Mary, called Magdalene, from whom seven demons had gone out, [3] and Joanna, the wife of Chuza, Herod's household manager, and Susanna, and many others, who provided for them out of their means.* (Luke 8:1-3)

2) When Jesus was crucified, the apostles left but we are told that some of Jesus' female disciples stayed by the cross to mourn:

> [55] *And many women who followed Jesus from Galilee, ministering to Him, were there looking on from afar, [56] among whom were Mary Magdalene, Mary the mother of James and Joses, and the mother of Zebedee's sons.* (Matthew 27:55-56)

3) On the day of Pentecost, which was the day the church was birthed, we read that both men and women joined:

> [14] *And believers were increasingly added to the Lord, multitudes of both men and women* (Acts 5:14)

All of the above scriptures show that women were certainly accepted into the early church, but what does the Bible teach about the specific point of women being church leaders?

A) In defence of women being church leaders, the main argument comes from the following scripture:

> *28 There is neither Jew nor Greek, there is neither slave nor free, there is neither male nor female; for you are all one in Christ Jesus.* (Galatians 3:28)

B) The contrary stance, however, is that men and women are to hold different roles in church. We find various scriptures supporting this view in the New Testament. The following scriptures reveal that deacons and bishops are to be male:

> *12 Let deacons be the husbands of one wife, ruling their children and their own houses well.* (1 Timothy 3:12)

> *This is a faithful saying: If a man desires the position of a bishop, he desires a good work. 2 A bishop then must be blameless, the husband of one wife, temperate, sober-minded, of good behavior, hospitable, able to teach;* (1 Timothy 3:1-2)

C) Perhaps the most controversial scriptures concerning the role of women are those which talk about female submission:

> *12 And I do not permit a woman to teach or to have authority over a man, but to be in silence.* (1 Timothy 2:12)

> *34 Let your women keep silent in the churches, for they are not permitted to speak; but they are to be submissive, as the law also says.* (1 Corinthians 14:34)

An important point which feeds into this discussion is that of the 'inerrancy' of scripture. If we believe that the 66 books of the Protestant Bible are the perfect Word of God, then we must take the above scriptures very seriously. If, on the other hand, we believe that Scripture is inspired but imperfect, then we can consider factors such as historical context when trying to understand the Bible, and perhaps take a more liberal view.

❧ 58 ❧

WHY IS LENT IMPORTANT?

10th February 2016

Today is Ash Wednesday, traditionally the first day of Lent. For me, Lent is about a spirit of gratitude for what God has done for me through His son Jesus Christ. The blessings that God affords us when we are devoted to Christ are so abundant. We gain hope that we will live forever, we are granted the forgiveness of sins, we have access to God through prayer and through His Word, and we have the hope of salvation and a place with Jesus in His kingdom in the life to come. None of this should be taken for granted.

During the Lenten season we remember the time when Jesus was tempted in the wilderness. We are told in Matthew 4 that Jesus fasted for 40 days and 40 nights before being tempted to rebel against God by the devil. So during lent we can think about the temptations that exist in our own lives, and we can commit to fasting – giving up some of our addictions – in order to focus more on our relationship with God through Jesus Christ.

Fasting is a personal thing between a person and God. We can prepare for fasting with prayer, asking God to place on our hearts the specific sacrifices we are to make during the Lenten season. Fasting is not something to show off about; indeed the Bible criticises any public display of fasting, which should really be done in secret (see Matthew 6:16-18).

My challenge to you if you are not a practising Christian is to dedicate some time during Lent to reading the Bible and exploring what God has to say about humility and sacrifice. Maybe try giving up one of your addictions for Lent (tea, coffee, smoking, sugar, meat, sex, etc), but don't do it so you can boast about it, do it to draw closer to God. In the Bible, prayer and fasting go together, so use this season to be prayerful and thankful for all that God has blessed you with. Reach out to God and He will hear you; as Jesus said, "knock and it shall be opened unto you" (Matthew 7:7).

May God bless you over the Lenten season!

✤ 59 ✤

THE TEN COMMANDMENTS

12th February 2016

According to the Bible, the Ten Commandments (or 'Decalogue') were given to Moses at Mount Sinai after he led the Jewish people out of their captivity in Egypt. In preparation for receiving the commandments, Moses fasted (no food or water) for 40 days and 40 nights.

The commandments were inscribed by God on two stone tablets and would represent the heart of the law that God gave to His chosen people Israel. It is of course no coincidence that Moses' fast was for the same length of time Jesus spent being tempted in the wilderness, which we now reflect upon during the Lenten season.

The Ten Commandments are listed twice in the Old Testament, in the book of Exodus and the book of Deuteronomy. I will list them below (from Exodus 20), and then briefly discuss the ways in which these commandments might be relevant to Christians today.

¹ And God spoke all these words, saying,

² "I am the Lord your God, who brought you out of the land of Egypt, out of the house of slavery.

³ "You shall have no other gods before me.

⁴ "You shall not make for yourself a carved image, or any likeness of anything that is in heaven above, or that is in the earth beneath, or that is in the water under the earth. ⁵ You shall not bow down to them or serve them, for I the Lord your God am a jealous God, visiting the iniquity of the fathers on the children to the third and the fourth generation of those who hate me, ⁶ but showing steadfast love to thousands of those who love me and keep my commandments.

⁷ "You shall not take the name of the Lord your God in vain, for the Lord will not hold him guiltless who takes his name in vain.

⁸ "Remember the Sabbath day, to keep it holy. ⁹ Six days you shall labor, and do all your work, ¹⁰ but the seventh day is a Sabbath to the Lord your God. On it you shall not do any work, you, or your son, or your daughter, your male servant, or your female servant, or your livestock, or the sojourner who is within your gates. ¹¹ For in six days the Lord made heaven and earth, the sea, and all that is in them, and rested on the seventh day. Therefore the Lord blessed the Sabbath day and made it holy.

12 "Honour your father and your mother, that your days may be long in the land that the Lord your God is giving you.

13 "You shall not murder.

14 "You shall not commit adultery.

15 "You shall not steal.

16 "You shall not bear false witness against your neighbour.

17 "You shall not covet your neighbour's house; you shall not covet your neighbour's wife, or his male servant, or his female servant, or his ox, or his donkey, or anything that is your neighbour's."

Most Christians believe the Ten Commandments are still relevant today. When asked by a man what he should do in order to inherit eternal life, Jesus replied that he should "keep the commandments" (Matthew 19:16-19).

Jesus stated that two commandments were the greatest - "thou shalt love the Lord thy God with all thy heart, and with all thy soul, and with all thy mind, and with all thy strength" (Mark 12:30) and "thou shalt love thy neighbour as thyself" (Mark 12:31). It is interesting that these two commandments do not specifically feature in the decalogue given to Moses and quoted above.

Some Christians believe that the Mosiac law no longer applies today because the teaching of Jesus 'superseded' it. Some believe that because of the New Covenant in Jesus' blood (1 Corinthians 11:25) we are no longer bound by the law, but are now living in a time of God's grace. This doesn't mean that there are no morals, but rather that God's law is now "written on our hearts" when we become believers in Christ (see the prophecy in Jeremiah 31:31-34).

Other Christians, such as those in the Eastern Orthodox Church, hold that the Ten Commandments are still applicable today. Indeed, in confession, penitents are asked to explain which of the commandments they have broken. In the Roman Catholic church it is believed that Jesus freed us from Jewish religious law, but that we are still required to keep the Ten Commandments. There are clearly a variety of views among Christians of differing denominations and persuasions who are practising today.

❧ 60 ❧

THE GRACE OF GOD

10th March 2016

Oh, most gracious Lord!

You are eternal, unfathomable; mighty beyond measure!

You have created all things and this complex universe is the work of Your hands. So far is Your divine knowledge from my shallow human understanding. I cannot comprehend Your ways, oh God!

In this wonderful mess of life, this perfect chaos, You reign; You are sovereign. Heaven and Earth are full of Your glory. Hosanna in the highest!

Thank You, Lord, for the many abundant blessings in my life. Thank You for my body, mind, and spirit. Thank You, Lord, for feeding me physically and spiritually. Thank You for Your forgiveness, Lord, and thank You for Your love. Thank You for the little things and the big things. Thank You for all that You do each day to bless me, help me, sustain me, and grow me.

Thank You, Lord, for listening to my supplications and my frustrations. My God, help me to be patient and to trust in You!

To my earthly mind, all is uncertain and mysterious, yet I believe You are in control. Your mercy is everything to me, Lord, and Your promises are so precious. Please, oh God, help me to pray and be mindful of the prayers I offer up to You. Know that I fear You, Lord, with a great fear!

I do love You, Lord God, even though the way ahead is uncertain. I trust, oh God, that You have clarity where I lack it. Please, Almighty God and Father, though I am a wretched sinner, guide me, and do not withhold Your love and mercy from me!

I crave Your comfort, Your security, Your love, Your hope, Your salvation. I long for You to bring peace to my soul.

Please, Lord, renew my mind and take away my anxieties. Let my faith be so strong, oh Lord, that I never question Your love or Your plan for my life. Be with me, oh God, at the sunrise and the sunset, throughout the day and throughout the night.

I wish to be blameless in Your sight, oh God. Teach me the way that pleases You, Lord, and do not let me stray from the righteous path. Correct me, Lord, when I do go astray. Forgive me, Lord, when I am selfish, conceited, forgetful, annoying, ignorant, or sinful.

Glory to my God, forever! For He has blessed us with a new and eternal covenant for the forgiveness of sins. Please remember Your blessed covenant, Lord, and forgive Your humble servant. Please, oh God, remember the suffering of Your only begotten Son, and do not let your anger burn against me.

Help me to be generous, oh God, and not selfish or greedy. Make my path straight, Lord, and help me to enter through the narrow gate. Help me to serve You all the days of my life.

May my offering of thanks and praise be acceptable to You, oh God, and may the grace of our Lord Jesus Christ, and the love of God, and the fellowship of the Holy Spirit, be with us all, evermore, Amen.

✦ 61 ✦

BEING HELD BY GOD

30th March 2016

Sometimes, life can be a real struggle. I know that I spent many years searching for peace, as I have reflected upon in my book *The Philosophy of a Mad Man* which is all about spiritual seeking. I used to immerse myself in Eastern philosophy as I tried to meditate my way to peace, at that time having had no revelation of the reality of God.

But Jesus said, "Ask, and it will be given to you; seek, and you will find; knock, and it will be opened to you." (Matthew 7:7). And God the Father said, "And you will seek Me and find Me, when you search for Me with all your heart." (Jeremiah 29:13).

And when it felt as though I had tried everything, when my soul was overwhelmed with restlessness, when I was banging my head against a spiritual brick wall; finally the Lord took pity on me and taught me about the gospel of grace; about the message of salvation through His Son Jesus Christ.

In Jesus, at last, there is peace.

It's not that suffering ends completely when you become a Christian. Even when we have found God, we still suffer. But Jesus is the lighthouse on the hillside that overlooks life's seas. He gives us assurance of God's love for us. Because of Jesus we know that God has chosen mercy for humankind, if only we will trust in Him.

I love these beautiful words from God:

> *"Because he has set his love upon Me, therefore I will deliver him;*
> *I will set him on high, because he has known My name.*
> *He shall call upon Me, and I will answer him;*
> *I will be with him in trouble;*
> *I will deliver him and honour him.*
> *With long life I will satisfy him,*
> *And show him My salvation."*
> (Psalm 91:14-16)

62

CHRISTOLOGICAL CONUNDRUMS

19th May 2016

I have spent some time recently studying Christian apologetics (defence of the faith) and have heard some Muslim scholars raising interesting questions about the Trinity and the dual (human & divine) nature of Christ. Here are a few thoughts.

One Muslim questioner was asking about Mark 11:12-14, which says the following:

> *12 Now the next day, when they had come out from Bethany, He was hungry. 13 And seeing from afar a fig tree having leaves, He went to see if perhaps He would find something on it. When He came to it, He found nothing but leaves, for it was not the season for figs. 14 In response Jesus said to it, "Let no one eat fruit from you ever again." And His disciples heard it.*

The questioner was suggesting that if Jesus is God, surely He could have made figs appear on the tree to satisfy His hunger. Why didn't He do so? Also, if Jesus is God, wouldn't He have known there were no figs on the tree before He even approached the tree?

I suppose what we're getting at here is the question of whether Jesus maintained qualities such as omnipotence, omniscience and omnipresence when He took on human form. It seems from this passage that He didn't, so are we really able to say He is fully God and fully man?

A different but associated question that has been puzzling me is this: Did Jesus will the crucifixion? There seem to me to be two conflicting scriptures here.

Firstly, John 10:17-18 (NKJV):

> **17** *"Therefore My Father loves Me, because I lay down My life that I may take it again.* **18** *No one takes it from Me, but I lay it down of Myself. I have power to lay it down, and I have power to take it again. This command I have received from My Father."*

Secondly, Luke 22:41-43 (NKJV), in which Jesus is praying to God the Father in anticipation of His crucifixion:

> **41** *And He was withdrawn from them about a stone's throw, and He knelt down and prayed,* **42** *saying, "Father, if it is Your will, take this cup away from Me; nevertheless not My will, but Yours, be done."* **43** *Then an angel appeared to Him from heaven, strengthening Him.* **44** *And being in agony, He*

prayed more earnestly. Then His sweat became like great drops of blood falling down to the ground...

Unless I am mistaken, it seems that in the first scripture Jesus is suggesting He has authority over His own life and death, but in the second scripture that He is dependent on the will of the Father. This is somewhat confusing.

63

CALVINISM AND
PREDESTINATION

24th May 2016

One of the most important concerns for any Christian is the doctrine of salvation (called "soteriology" by academics). The subject raises important questions: What is salvation? How do I get saved? Can I ever lose my salvation?

In this brief article, I want to look at salvation from the point of view of Calvinism and the associated doctrine of predestination. Calvinism is the Protestant school of thought associated with the reformed theologian John Calvin. Predestination is the idea that long before we are born, God decides whether or not we will be one of His "elect" who will be saved by His grace during our earthly lives.

I want to discuss five key points of Calvinism, and criticise them with specific reference to my own ideas about free will. I am not going to include Scripture references here, but if you want to know whereabouts in the Bible the Calvinists get their ideas from there are many articles available online that elucidate. And please note, I am not claiming to get my ideas from the Bible.

1. Total Depravity

This is the idea that due to original sin we are born sinners and that during our human life we are slaves to sin, which affects our minds, bodies, wills, and emotions.

I have always thought that original sin is a strange idea; that through the disobedient actions of God's first created man we have all become sinners from our very conception. I know that I am in a sense separate from God, as clearly I am living through an embodied experience with a human conscious-ness, whereas I believe God has attributes that I don't possess, such as omnipotence, omniscience, and omnipresence. But Christians tend to understand sin as disobedience, rather than mere separateness.

As I have argued in other posts, the ultimate truth is that it is not possible for humans to have fallen away from God, as God is, and always has been, in control of everything that happens. We are not free to act in any way that is contrary to the will of God, as God is everywhere. This is a simple attribute of the nature of God.

We do possess the *illusion* of free will, as God is able to hide His ultimate nature from us during our earthly lives so that many do not realise that we are like puppets in a puppet show and God is the cosmic puppeteer. When I breathe, move, think, grow, digest, or act in any way, it is because God is controlling these activities in the *present moment*. God is a living God – He didn't create the universe and then sit back and watch it unfold, but rather He is actively sustaining and developing this vast universe which is not ontologically different from Him. God is all that exists and therefore nothing can happen outside of His will. It seems to me that the idea of Total Depravity in Calvinism ignores this reality.

2. Unconditional Election

This is the idea that we can do nothing to earn our salvation. From a certain perspective this makes a lot of sense to me as if God is always in control, then we do not have free will, and therefore how could we possibly do anything freely to warrant election or damnation? It makes more sense that our cosmic puppeteer would choose whether we are saved based on His will, rather that our own free will which is illusory.

The whole purpose of creation is for God to experience possibility (His own vast nature) in all its fullness; the yin and yang; light and darkness; good and evil; heaven and hell. I have heard it said by one Calvinist that this is indeed the purpose of creation, but to me it seems terribly unfair that some people would have to suffer in hell just so that God can experience that part of His nature.

I have speculated in my book *Ultimate Truth: God Beyond Religion* that I believe God is ultimately merciful and would never let anyone suffer too much, although I believe the Calvinist would argue that those who are not among the elect are damned to hell for all eternity. Would a merciful God really punish people in this way, even though they have done nothing freely to warrant such treatment? It is not for me to judge God, of course, but nevertheless I think it's an important point.

3. Limited Atonement

This is the idea that Jesus died only for the elect. If life is God's game and we are all puppets in God's hands, then I can see that it is possible that as part of the game Jesus came to shed His blood as an atoning sacrifice for the sins of men, as most Christians believe. The Arminians believe that Jesus died for *everyone in the whole world*, and that each individual has a free choice as to whether to repent and believe and in doing so to get saved.

The Calvinist idea that Jesus died only for the elect seems to make sense only if we embrace the idea that we don't have free will and that God is controlling all things. You see, if God is in control, then He knows who will be saved, so therefore it becomes possible to say Jesus died only for them. Free will is again the central issue here.

4. Irresistible Grace

According to Calvinism, when God calls the elect, they cannot resist. The implication here is clearly that they don't have free will. But what confuses me here about the Calvinist position is that they argue the Gospel message is offered by God to *all people*. I would have to argue that because God is in control, those who reject the Gospel are only doing so by the will of God. Another problem is that in reality there are millions who will live and die without ever hearing the Gospel (unless, of course, God brings the Gospel to them in another realm that we don't know about), so in ultimate reality they are damned by the will of God who has not chosen to impart His irresistible grace to them. We might call this "irresistible damnation" (I believe it is also called "double predestination").

5. Perseverance of the Saints

The idea here is that the elect are eternally saved and can do nothing to lose their salvation. This is a very comforting thought, but in reality our present moment living God can change His mind in any moment, and as He is in control of all things, there is always the possibility that our destiny could change. It may well be that God does choose to save the elect eternally, but we shouldn't deny that it is within God's power to change His mind at any moment.

Conclusion

The central problem within Calvinism, and I would argue within the whole of Christian theology, is free will. With an omnipresent God there can be no free will (the two ideas are logically incompatible) and therefore Calvinists are misguided if they combine their doctrine of election, which implies a God who is in control, with the idea that we are free to act independently of God's will (which is the very definition of what free will is).

64

WHO ARE THE HERETICS?

26th June 2016

I'm lucky that there's a library about ten minutes walk from where I live in south west London. It's not a huge library; I would guess there are about 30-40 books in the Christianity section which is where I was looking when I visited earlier this week.

So I was lucky, then, to find a book that really caught my attention: 'Reformation: A World in Turmoil' by Andrew Atherstone. The book is an excellent guide to the Reformation and has already provided me with much food for thought even though I'm currently only about half way through.

One of the things that is standing out for me as I read this book is the diversity of opinions that different Christians held about the key doctrinal issues of the faith. During the Reformation there were many believers who were tortured, burned at the stake, beheaded, drowned, or otherwise executed, for holding opinions that differed from those who were in power in a particular region at a particular time.

I want to quote a short section from page 147 of the book on the subject of heresy and then make a few comments below. I would love to get your thoughts in the comments at the bottom of this post.

In his treatise, *On Heretics*, [Sebastian] Castellio argued that Christians spent far too much time arguing about unprofitable doctrines like the Trinity, the work of Christ, predestination, free will, angels, and the immortality of the soul. He maintained that such debates were irrelevant since salvation was achieved not by doctrinal precision but through faith in Christ, as tax-collectors and prostitutes realized in New Testament times. Castellio went further and asserted that it was futile to punish "heresy", because Christians could not agree among themselves which views were heretical. Surveying the bewildering multitude of Christian opinions in evidence across sixteenth-century Europe, he wrote:

> *There is hardly one of all the sects, which today are without number, which does not hold the others to be heretics. So that if in one city or region you are esteemed to be a true believer, in the next you will be esteemed a heretic. So that if anyone today wants to live he must have as many faiths and religions as there are cities or sects, just as a man who travels through the lands has to change his money from day to day...*

Castellio looked for an emphasis upon Christian morality rather than doctrinal correctness, and maintained: "It would be better to let a hundred, even a thousand heretics live than to put a decent man to death under pretence of heresy."

In our current age of YouTube videos and the blogosphere there are still debates raging around all the same issues that were being discussed vehemently in Castellio's day. The plurality of beliefs amongst Christians has not decreased. There are thousands of different denominations in the church today. We may not be burning people at the stake for their beliefs, but we are still arguing about the same doctrinal issues.

I wonder how God views all these different beliefs? Is it really true that just a small number of Christians will be able to "enter through the narrow gate" and be saved? Or is it arrogance to assume that one person's views about, say, the Trinity, are going to leave them damned to hell while another's views will carry them to heaven?

If it is true that the Bible is the infallible Word of God, as many Christians believe, does it really follow that there is one correct interpretation of Scripture, or should we be more liberal in allowing for different beliefs and interpretations within the church?

Castellio's view was that we should put morality first. This suggests to me that he believed we should be more concerned about our conduct as Christians than the minutiae of doctrinal differences. Perhaps a good Christian is able to empathise with the views of others, putting himself in their shoes and understanding that despite being different, their opinion may not be heresy in God's eyes.

65

THE MOST SERIOUS OF GAMES

9th July 2016

I am acutely aware of the seriousness of faith. The major Abrahamic religions (Judaism, Christianity, and Islam) are all concerned with salvation, and how we can be "right with God". If there is a God who has created this vast universe, as I am convinced there is, then His power to bring salvation or damnation is of the utmost importance and we are right to fear Him.

It is this fear of God which has led me to study religion in depth. In my adult life I have made it my mission to understand more about God and religion, and to try to ascertain what truth is and how I can live in the best possible way. I'm still learning, and the more I explore the more I realise the vast range of opinions that exist in matters that are of huge theological importance.

If heaven and hell exist, and if only one religious path leads to salvation, then many billions of people will be damned to hell. The reason I find this concept difficult is because I believe God is completely in control of our lives and our destinies. The idea that God would judge people for actions which He has freely undertaken (to unfold our lives in a certain way) is problematic as we can have done nothing freely to warrant God's wrath. As a caveat to this, I must point out that it is not my place to judge God, and I don't deny He has the power and authority to do whatever He chooses, even if damning certain people to hell might seem cruel or unfair to my human understanding.

I find it difficult to understand those who believe that God is omnipotent, omniscient, and omnipresent, but at the same time argue that we have free will. It is so clear to me that we do not have free will. We do not take the decision to be born. We do not choose to grow from nothing into babies and then toddlers and then teenagers and then adults. We do not choose the colour of our skin or our eyes. We do not choose how our organs are arranged in our bodies. We do not choose our parents, or our siblings. We do not choose to make our hearts beat, or our blood flow. We do not choose to grow our nails or our hair. We do not choose our dreams when we sleep. We do not choose to digest our food and drink.

In the same way, we don't choose which thoughts will arise in our minds. If you believe you are in control of your thoughts then tell me, what is a thought? How do you make thoughts arise in your mind? What will you be thinking about in an hour's time, or at this time next year? If you say thoughts are caused by your subconscious, then please explain what this subconscious is and who or what is in control of it. If you think that you are merely a product of evolution, then please explain what is the cause of this evolution. If you believe we exist due to a set of mathematical laws, then please explain why these laws exist. And tell me, why does anything exist at all?

What causes the seed to grow into a flower? What causes the tree to sprout up from the earth and grow its branches and its fruit? My friend, when you pray for good weather, a fruitful harvest, or a new job, are you not praying to a God who is in control? Do you really not see that God is in control of all things?

And yet still, there are those who attempt to argue that God only does good things; that He is not in control of your ailments and your diseases; your very life and death. There are those who argue that God blesses them with a husband or wife, or a tasty meal, or a new job, but then deny that it is also God who causes the divorce, or the food poisoning, or the redundancy. Friend, can't you see the hypocrisy in this way of thinking? Surely you know, if you are honest with yourself, that God is in control of all those things which you call "good" and all those things which you call "evil".

I hear you arguing that your holy scriptures talk about the devil as the cause of evil in the world. Friend, do not be naive. Have you really thought in depth about what the devil is? I would like to know some attributes of this creature. Where does he dwell exactly? Does he live within a creaturely body?

Is he able to somehow insert thoughts into your mind? Surely he would have to be omnipresent in order to control our thoughts. What are his powers? What does he control in contrast with what God controls? Please, give me some insights into Satan and his powers, and let those insights be rational!

If the devil exists, he must be under God's control, as everything is. To argue against this would be to deny God's omnipresence. The myth of the fall, and the entire Christian story, are based on the idea that we have free will, which we do not. How can it be said that we are sinners, when all of our sin is willed by God?

If you're still not convinced, my friends, I'd like to invite you to undertake a simple exercise. Take a sheet of paper, divide it into three columns, and label the columns 'God', 'Satan', and 'Human'. Then under each of those headings proceed to list the things of which each of the three persons is in control. We might call this 'The Will Game'. You could even put certain activities into more than one column. My intention is to encourage you to think deeply about the cause of activity in existence, in the microcosm and the macrocosm.

Now I do not wish to offend my Almighty God and Father, to whom I kneel in prayer each and every day. I do not wish to offend the God who has power to make me suffer in every moment for all eternity. Heavens, that is the last thing I wish to do! I am driven to speak the truth in accordance with my convictions, and may you, my friends, persuade me otherwise if I am wrong! I cannot argue that God is in control, as I have done here, and then deny that my convictions come from God. God must be willing me to write this article or I wouldn't be doing so. The Lord knows full well that I am merely a puppet in His hands!

Perhaps I am in dangerous territory. Could it be that by speaking so openly about the truth that I perceive, I am participating in my own downfall? This worries me greatly. I don't know whether the Christian story is so beloved by God that anyone who questions it is guilty of a grave sin. I can believe that the Christian story is God's game that He has chosen to play over the last two thousand years, and maybe it is a great sin to shed light on the errors and inconsistencies in this great story which has produced so many saints and martyrs.

I write not to argue against God but to convey what God has revealed to me. I am a lonely voice in a world where either people have forsaken God in their atheism or they hold blindly to a set of doctrines and defend them at all costs. People are quick to say who will be saved and who will be damned, but I do not claim to have such knowledge, despite what any particular scripture says! I have a hope that God is ultimately merciful to every sentient being, and I do pray that God chooses mercy over damnation for all of us, regardless of our beliefs - beliefs which He has bestowed upon us!

Lord, forgive me if I have sinned in writing this article. You know my heart. You know that I hate doing anything that annoys or angers you. I know that if this article speaks to anyone, it will be through your Spirit working in the minds of those who read. I ask, Lord, that you would show these people only what is true, and that you would save their minds from any thoughts you would consider blasphemous. May your truth and your will prosper, Lord!

66

TONY THE ALCOHOLIC (A CASE STUDY)

9th August 2016

Consider this scenario, if you will. An alcoholic is in court owing to a drunken rampage he went on where he threw a dustbin into the window of a local store, smashing the window and injuring a young lady who was restocking the shelves near the window at the time. The young lady wishes to press charges, but the man is denying responsibility.

You might naturally wonder, how can this man deny responsibility for his actions? Well, let us explore a possible line of defence. The man (let's call him Tony) has been an alcoholic for many years and has been in and out of rehab, has attended counselling and Alcoholics Anonymous meetings, but has been unable to break the habit.

Additionally, Tony's father was an alcoholic, and his grandfather on his father's side too. The defence, which Tony and his lawyer are arguing, is that he is not responsible for the alcoholism which led to the incident involving the young lady in the store. His defence rests upon some evidence that was presented showing that there is a gene in Tony's DNA that is linked to alcoholism.

The question at the heart of the matter is obvious: To what extent are we responsible for our actions, and to what extent are our actions determined by prior events or our genetic makeup? And I want to add another, perhaps less commonly discussed but crucial question to our discussion: What is God's role in all of this and how does that affect the debate?

The idea of determinism, which is popular in modern science, leads us to sympathise with Tony and conclude that his drunken actions are the result not of his own free will, but of a tendency which he inherited. This leads us into murky waters, as responsibility can't then be placed on Tony's father or grandfather for the same reasons; they all simply inherited the troublesome gene. It is difficult, then, to apportion blame to anyone.

Many people would argue that determinism and free will are compatible and are both important components which contribute to our behaviour. But anyone who wrestles with where exactly we should draw the line between the two would have to acknowledge that it is a highly problematic task. Judges and Jurys in court rooms naturally have to mull over such dilemmas all the time, and I can imagine decisions of this nature must be agonising as the arguments can be compelling from both sides.

In a similar vein, theologians argue about the distinction between God's will and human free will. This is the same problem, and raises the same questions, only it is framed slightly differently: Where does God's responsibility end and human free will begin?

In my latest book, entitled *Ultimate Truth: God Beyond Religion*, I present arguments to the effect that God is in control of everything that happens in existence. I suggest that God is omnipresent, which means that nothing exists outside of Him (or put another way, God is all there is). Following this line of argument, we would have to say that God is in control of all activity in existence, including all human action, whether we would consider that action to be 'good' or 'evil'.

Returning to our discussion of Tony the alcoholic, might we then say that because God was in control of his thoughts, words, and actions on the night of his drunken rampage he is off the hook and not liable? If God is always in control, can we ever really hold someone responsible for crimes they are supposed to have committed?

67

JERRY BRIDGES AND GOD'S SOVEREIGNTY

12th August 2016

Jerry Bridges is fast becoming one of my favourite Christian authors. In recent weeks I have read two books by Bridges on Christian living, entitled *The Pursuit of Holiness* and *The Practice of Godliness*. These books are written in a simple, accessible style, and are full of quotations from Scripture, so advocates of sola scriptura will not be disappointed.

Bridges contributed a chapter to the book I'm currently reading. Entitled *Still Sovereign*, the book is a compilation of fourteen articles by different authors defending the sovereignty of God from a Calvinistic perspective. The chapter penned by Bridges is entitled "Does Divine Sovereignty Make a Difference in Everyday Life?" and is my favourite chapter of the book so far (I still have a few chapters left to read).

What I like about Bridges' chapter is that his thoughts about divine sovereignty line up with my own beliefs in many ways. Throughout the chapter, Bridges quotes from Scripture to demonstrate the plentiful evidence for God's sovereignty in every aspect of life.

First off, we see from the Book of James that God's will is active even in the mundane tasks we carry out in our everyday lives:

> *Now listen, you who say, "Today or tomorrow we will go to this or that city, spend a year there, carry on business and make money." Why, you do not even know what will happen tomorrow. What is your life? You are a mist that appears for a little while and then vanishes. Instead, you ought to say, "If it is the Lord's will, we will live and do this or that." As it is, you boast and brag. All such boasting is evil.* (James 4:13-16)

Bridges then explains how many of us say the phrase 'God willing' in passing when we're talking about our plans, even in secular society. But most people don't realise that it really is true that nothing in our daily lives happens apart from the will of God. To not acknowledge this is described as 'evil' in James' epistle.

Jesus himself also spoke about matters that touch on the issue of divine sovereignty. Here's a quote that Bridges uses from the Book of Matthew:

> *Do not be afraid of those who kill the body but cannot kill the soul. Rather, be afraid of the One who can destroy both soul and body in hell. Are not two sparrows sold for a penny? Yet*

not one of them will fall to the ground apart from the will of your Father. And even the very hairs of your head are all numbered. So don't be afraid; you are worth more than many sparrows. (10:28-31)

I love what Jesus says here about the very hairs on our head being numbered, as it shows how God is present even in the tiniest detail of our lives. I often ponder how awesome it is that tiny insects behave in such complex ways (e.g. spiders who weave their webs and ants who build their tunnels and hills). In all the minutiae of life, as well as all the grand thunderstorms and earthquakes, God is in control.

Several pages later, Bridges makes an important confession: "It is of little comfort to me to know that God loves me if He is not in control of the events of my life." This saying is a breath of fresh air! I get so much comfort myself knowing that God is in control of my life. But there is a flip-side to this knowledge, which Bridges doesn't mention, which is that if all is under God's control, there is no hiding place or escape route should God be angry with us and wish to punish us, as He did the Israelites on many occasions in Old Testament times.

Bridges goes on to discuss God's sovereignty over people, and states "...the concept of divine sovereignty over people seems to destroy the free will of humans and make them no more than puppets on God's stage." This should bring a smile to the face of anyone who is familiar with my own writings and philosophy, as I believe this is precisely the truth of the matter and we shouldn't shy away from it! It seems to me that so many theologians come desperately close to admitting we have no free will, but shy away from ever stating this explicitly, because of the implications in terms of the key Christian message about human responsibility for sin. It has been clear to me for many years that even those things we do which might be considered sinful are under God's control. We *are* those puppets. I have never read a theologian brave enough to admit it, as it means we have to look at the fall of man and the atoning sacrifice of Christ in a wholly new light (more about this in my book, *Ultimate Truth: God Beyond Religion*).

More scriptural evidence that God controls our lives can be found in Proverbs 21:1, which states, "The king's heart is in the hand of the Lord, he directs it like a watercourse wherever he pleases." This is true of kings and other world leaders and it is also true of all other human beings. As that famous Sunday School song goes, "He's got the whole world in His hands."

If we are going to truly accept the sovereignty of God then we must be prepared to confess He is in control of both good and evil. It seems Bridges acknowledges this and he quotes many scriptures which support this view. He also states, "...as his children we can be sure that all evil intended against us by other people is either permitted or restrained as he chooses." Bridges proceeds to explain:

> God's sovereignty over people does not mean we do not experience pain and suffering. It means that God is in control of our pain and suffering, and that he has in mind a beneficial purpose for it. There is no such thing as pain without a purpose for the child of God. (p 301)

In the human 'dimension' of reality, it still seems as though we do have free will, as we think our individual thoughts and make decisions to go to certain places and do certain things. But I believe that sense of free will is an illusion; it is a mode of mind that is completely under the sovereign control of God. Nevertheless, because we do feel that we are free, we should act responsibly. While he doesn't completely deny free will, Bridges agrees with me on this point and states,

> ...it must be emphasised that belief in divine sovereignty in the everyday affairs of our lives should never cause us to act imprudently or irresponsibly. The Scriptures repeatedly teach us our responsibility for prudent actions. The Book of Proverbs, for example, is filled with this type of teaching. (p 303)

We should note the 'compatibilist paradox' here – God is in control of all action and yet we are still encouraged in Scripture to make prudent decisions. The way I like to describe this is that *whatever you do, God is doing through you.*

In conclusion, then, there is ample evidence in Scripture that God is in control of every aspect of our lives. I believe that we can come to know this through intuition, contemplation, and reflection. I have written extensively on the subject of free will on my blog and in my books, and it is wonderful and refreshing to read the perspective of Jerry Bridges, whose views on the subject are not a million miles away from my own.

❦ 68 ❦

COUNSELLING AND FAITH

7th September 2016

As many of you know I have been through a rather "turbulent" mental health journey over the last decade. I'm actually doing pretty well at the moment and next month will mark three and half years since I was last in hospital. This has been the longest period of sound mental health for me since my first hospital admission in 2007.

I am taking medication in the form of an injection every two weeks (and a couple of tablets morning and evening to help deal with the side effects from the injection). Compared to some of the medication I've been on my current regime is pretty manageable, although I'm still experiencing side effects which are inhibiting and unpleasant.

I'm so grateful to God and I thank Him each day for the abundant blessings in my life. I have a roof over my head, food and drink, Internet access, support from my local Mind (a mental health charity), and I recently started to attend some low-cost counselling, which is proving to be very helpful and is what I want to focus on in this article.

I have had three counselling sessions with Yvonne (not her real name) and each one has been interesting, challenging, and thought-provoking. I'm no stranger to talking therapies; in the past I have attended private psychotherapy, group CBT, one-to-one CBT, and Christian counselling. I also tried psychodynamic counselling once but it was a bit like trying to interact with a brick wall so I gave up after a single session. I am mature enough now that I generally have a good idea of what is going to be helpful and what isn't.

I identify as a Christian, even though there are aspects of Christian theology that trouble me and often cause me to question the faith. I try to live out the two great commandments identified by Jesus – to love the Lord with all my heart, soul, mind, and strength, and to love my neighbour as myself. I try to make these two commandments the focus of my life, and part of the reason I am attending counselling is to try to understand myself in a deeper way so that I can be of greater assistance to others.

To be honest, I have been in two minds about whether it's a good idea to attend 'secular' counselling (and by that I mean counselling where one's faith is not necessarily central to the process). I have been worried that when it comes to talking about my beliefs, there may be certain things that are profoundly important to me, such as the way I understand God, Jesus, or the Bible, that my therapist might not be able to relate to. I worry about this before every session. Having a personal relationship with God is such a wonderful thing, but can seem like madness to someone who doesn't have such a relationship (See 1 Corinthians 1:18).

I haven't held back from talking about Jesus in my sessions with Yvonne so far. And I have been pleasantly surprised by her response when matters of faith have arisen. Yvonne is a true professional, and works hard to help me to understand my own beliefs, behaviours, and values, without being critical or judgmental in any way. And to me, this goes to show that even for people of faith, counselling can be a wonderful thing.

With counselling, it's always important to remember it is a two-way relationship. There are things that the client can teach the counsellor as well as things that the counsellor can teach the client, and of course the ultimate truth is that God is using these sessions to teach both client and counsellor. Every counsellor is a flawed human being, as is every client. Everyone has gifts to give and lessons to learn.

Therapy has been life-changing for me in the past and with Yvonne it is proving to be life-changing once again. Attending therapy doesn't mean that you're more broken than everyone else, it means that you have a desire to grow and develop and understand your personality and your strengths and weaknesses in a deeper way.

I suppose there are those Christians who might argue that all we need for our personal and spiritual development is contained within the pages of Scripture, and if we are guided by the Holy Spirit when reading the Bible then all the truth we need will be revealed. Is it a kind of idolatry to attend counselling with a secular counsellor who doesn't necessarily share your faith? Does seeing a secular counsellor mean you are putting your trust in human beings rather than in the inerrant and infallible Word of God?

2 Timothy 3:16 says "All Scripture is given by inspiration of God, and is profitable for doctrine, for reproof, for correction, for instruction in righteousness". This verse shows us that all Scripture is important, but does that mean that *only* Scripture is important? Does the Bible support the idea that counselling could be beneficial to us on our spiritual journeys?

The book of Proverbs has a lot to say about this. For example, Proverbs 13:10 reads "Through insolence comes nothing but strife, but wisdom is with those who receive counsel." Proverbs 15:22 reads "Without consultation, plans are frustrated, but with many counsellors they succeed." And Proverbs 12:15 gives further guidance: "The way of a fool is right in his own eyes, but a wise man is he who listens to counsel."

It could be argued that in the above quotations, counsel means 'Godly counsel', and this can only come from believing Christians or the Bible. But might it be the case that God also uses secular influences to help us to grow on our spiritual journeys, to help us deal with pain and abuse and hardship, and to grow in wisdom and understanding? Even if Jesus is the way, the truth, and the life, are there still things we can learn from non-believers?

I will end with a short poem and I will leave it to you to make up your own mind as to whether secular counselling is profitable or sinful. This is something I must work out for myself as well.

Approach all things with open mind,
All have gifts to which we're blind,
Be sensitive to others' cries,
Others too are also wise.

(Author Unknown)

69

WHAT IS THE HOLY SPIRIT?

21st October 2016

Christians believe in one God in three persons; Father, Son, and Holy Spirit. Having watched a few debates between Christians and Muslims about the Trinity, I'm aware that it's a concept that can at times be confusing. For instance, while Jesus walked the earth He prayed to God the Father. But if Jesus is fully God (as is stated in the Chalcedonian Creed), is there a sense in which He was praying to Himself? Also, did Jesus maintain attributes we normally associate with God (such as omnipotence and omniscience) during His earthly life?

As well as attempting to define the role of Jesus within the Trinity, the ecumenical councils in Christian history have also tried to define the Holy Spirit. In this article I would like to look at Scripture and make a few points and raise a few questions about what the Holy Spirit is and how it operates.

Well, I've barely begun and already we have a problem. I just described the Holy Spirit as 'it'. Christians believe the Spirit is a *person* and would normally refer to it as 'He'. There are many scriptures that support the idea that the Spirit is an agent with His own volition. Here are a couple of examples:

> *But when the Helper comes, whom I will send to you from the Father, the Spirit of truth, who proceeds from the Father, he will bear witness about me.* (John 15:26 ESV)

> *When the Spirit of truth comes, he will guide you into all the truth, for he will not speak on his own authority, but whatever he hears he will speak, and he will declare to you the things that are to come.* (John 16:13 ESV)

These scriptures show Jesus talking to His disciples about the Holy Spirit and it is clear from what Jesus says that the Spirit can bear witness, guide them, speak, and declare; all activities that we would associate with personal agency. The above scriptures are from the New Testament, but references to the Holy Spirit in the Old Testament are numerous as well. For example:

> *The earth was without form and void, and darkness was over the face of the deep. And the Spirit of God was hovering over the face of the waters.* (Genesis 1:2 ESV)

> *Then he said to me, "This is the word of the Lord to Zerubbabel: Not by might, nor by power, but by my Spirit, says the Lord of hosts.* (Zechariah 4:6 ESV)

In John 14:26 (in the New Testament) the Holy Spirit is referred to as the "comforter" (or "advocate" or "helper" depending on the translation) which clearly distinguishes Him as a person in contrast to any concept of the Spirit as an impersonal force.

So if the Spirit is a person, like God the Father and God the Son, does it make sense to pray to Him? Well, I can find little evidence of prayer directly to the Holy Spirit in the Bible. Instead, we are told to pray *in* the Spirit (see Ephesians 6:18). But there is some confusion about this among Christians. I have often heard Christians praying the phrase "Come, Holy Spirit", which I suppose is a prayer to Him. In my experience, when praying or worshiping with a group of believers, there can be a real sense of the presence of God which we might also describe as the presence of the Holy Spirit.

So we could say that the Holy Spirit is a feeling of the presence of God during prayer and worship. Christians also ask for the assistance of the Spirit when studying the Bible. This implies that the Spirit is directly linked to our minds and has the power to speak to us and give us knowledge and understanding. It could perhaps be said that the Spirit is God's way of communicating with us – the link between God the Father in heaven and the human mind here on Earth.

Perhaps the most well-known incidence in the Bible of the Holy Spirit working is on the Day of Pentecost; a historical event still celebrated by Christians today. We find in Acts 2 the following passage:

When the Day of Pentecost had fully come, they were all with one accord in one place. And suddenly there came a sound from heaven, as of a rushing mighty wind, and it filled the whole house where they were sitting. Then there appeared to them divided tongues, as of fire, and one sat upon each of them. And they were all filled with the Holy Spirit and began to speak with other tongues, as the Spirit gave them utterance. (Acts 2:1-4 NKJV)

We see from this passage that an aspect of the Holy Spirit is that it can imbue certain supernatural powers into believers; in this case, speaking in tongues. In 1 Corinthians, the apostle Paul explains the role of the Holy Spirit in more depth and describes the different gifts that believers can expect to receive from Him:

Brothers and sisters, I want you to know about the gifts of the Holy Spirit. You know that at one time you were unbelievers. You were somehow drawn away to worship statues of gods that couldn't even speak. So I want you to know that no one who is speaking with the help of God's Spirit says, "May Jesus be cursed." And without the help of the Holy Spirit no one can say, "Jesus is Lord."

There are different kinds of gifts. But they are all given to believers by the same Spirit. There are different ways to serve. But they all come from the same Lord. There are different ways the Spirit works. But the same God is working in all these ways and in all people.

The Holy Spirit is given to each of us in a special way. That is for the good of all. To some people the Spirit gives a message of wisdom. To others the same Spirit gives a message of knowledge. To others the same Spirit gives faith. To others that one Spirit gives gifts of healing. To others he gives the power to do miracles. To others he gives the ability to prophesy. To others he gives the ability to tell the spirits apart. To others he gives the ability to speak in different kinds of languages they had not known before. And to still others he gives the ability to explain what was said in those languages. All the gifts are produced by one and the same Spirit. He gives gifts to each person, just as he decides. (1 Corinthians 12: 1-11 NIV)

One of the most well-known scriptures that references the Holy Spirit is Matthew 3:16, where Jesus is being baptised. The scripture describes Jesus coming out of the water and the Spirit of God "descending like a dove and alighting on Him". This is a very visual description of the Spirit but it is clearly a metaphor so shouldn't be taken too literally. Nevertheless we see here another insight into how the person of the Holy Spirit acts.

Despite what has been explored in this article, there remains a mysterious element to the Holy Spirit, for me at least. When I am reading a novel, or a book about history, and I receive understanding – is that the Holy Spirit working in me? Does the Holy Spirit leave me when I am not engaged in prayer or Bible reading or other spiritual activities? Does the Spirit come and go, and is the Spirit absent from all non-Christians? What is the substance or essence of the Spirit, and how is the Spirit involved with thoughts and feelings?

I suppose I think of God as a spiritual being, meaning that His essence is spirit rather than anything physical. I also believe God is omnipresent, which means His spirit (or He as Spirit) is everywhere without exception in existence. One scripture that supports this idea is Acts 17:28, which says "For in Him we live, and move, and have our being". It seems to me that this scripture only makes sense if God is a spiritual being. But it does beg the question – how might we describe God the Father ontologically as *distinct* from God the Holy Spirit?

Hopefully I have touched upon some of the most important aspects of the Holy Spirit as revealed in Scripture in this article (which is by no means exhaustive). In any case, it seems that there are some questions about the nature of the Holy Spirit that Scripture does not answer explicitly. But then maybe God is happy for there to be an element of mystery in relation to this subject. Like so many of God's mysteries, it may be a subject that only fully makes sense when we have passed on from our earthly existence.

⁂ 70 ⁂

MY GUILTY AMERICANO

22nd October 2016

As a Christian and a person who believes it's right to try to live in pursuit of holiness and to practise godliness wherever possible, I sometimes find myself experiencing moral dilemmas concerning how to act appropriately in certain situations.

I believe that telling the truth is very important. Sometimes it can be tempting to tell a white lie. When I'm shopping in my local supermarket and the cashier asks me "Is it your day off today?", part of me wants to simply reply "yes" and pick up my shopping and be on my way. But I don't want to lie. The truth is I'm out of work due to health issues and to be true to myself I feel I need to explain this, even in a brief conversation with someone I don't know.

Why does it matter? Well, in my experience, even little white lies come back to haunt us. What happens when I see the cashier again the following week and she starts to open up a conversation by asking, "So, what do you do for a living?". Either I tell another lie and get myself into deeper trouble, or I have to explain that I was lying the week before. The situation becomes complicated. It's so much better just to be honest with everyone from the outset and to keep a clear conscience. Speaking the truth means peace of mind.

I do sometimes slip up, and I think sometimes God tests me by putting me in situations where my conscience is tested. The other day I was in a coffee shop ordering an Americano, and as a regular customer I know the price is always £2.55. I saw the price come up on the till as £2.20, and so I figured the barista had made a mistake. I decided to be honest and mentioned that it's normally £2.55, but he said he realised that but felt like doing me a favour.

For a moment I thought this was a friendly gesture from a barista who I see often and who knows my order. But immediately after I accepted the discount I felt a sense of guilt consume me. All of a sudden I was in two minds: Do I go back and pay the difference and explain that it feels morally wrong to take the discount? Or do I accept that the discount was the barista's responsibility and go happily on my way?

The guy was trying to do me a favour, but by breaking the rules he was causing trouble for me (by testing my conscience) and for himself. What if his manager found out he was discounting certain people's coffee on a whim? How would the person next in line to me feel about this partiality? What happens the next time I go in for a coffee and he serves me – will he feel obliged to offer the discount every time?

I feel I shouldn't have accepted the discount, but it all happened so quickly. I feel like I need to be more on my guard in order to keep a clear conscience and know the difference between right and wrong in everyday circumstances and situations.

For some people, telling white lies is an everyday thing, and I don't know how they live with themselves. For instance, yesterday I was in a pub and there was a man sitting alone near me having a few pints. His phone rang and I heard him explaining to the caller that he was in a meeting. I don't think I could tell a lie like that in good conscience.

I think that when we tell the truth, good things happen. When I am open with people about my mental health problems it allows for a deeper level of understanding and intimacy with people than if I were to hide the truth or tell a lie. Being honest and vulnerable also has the effect of tackling stigma, as people realise it's possible for someone to have a mental illness and still be friendly, mature, warm, and intelligent.

Some may argue that accepting a 35 pence discount on my Americano is no big deal. Perhaps it isn't a big deal, but I am determined to live with a clear conscience and to do all I can to be honest, for my own peace of mind and to ensure I am doing my best to love my neighbour as myself, as Jesus instructed. The next time someone tries to do me a favour in an underhand way, I pray I will act with conscience and do that right thing, not the easy thing.

71

GOD'S OMNIPRESENCE AND THE INCARNATION

23rd October 2016

I often hear Christians speaking of what a miraculous and wonderful thing it is that God chose to enter into His own creation in the person of Jesus Christ in the event known as the Incarnation.

The problem with this notion is that it implies that God is normally somehow separated from creation. How can this be? The God I believe in is omnipresent and pervades and sustains the whole of creation. The universe and everything in it is part of His being.

Isn't it God who grows the trees and flowers, moves the planets by His power, and grows the hair on our heads? How could He do these things if He isn't present everywhere all of the time?

I cannot conceive of a God who is somehow separate from certain parts of existence as this would imply a limit to His power and to the very things, ontologically speaking, that make Him God. I feel uncomfortable with the idea that before and after the Incarnation God is somehow existing in a place outside of the world in which we live.

Surely, as believers, we know intuitively that God is everywhere. If, for instance, I pray to God asking Him to plant me in a great church, isn't the implication that He is in control of my actions?

God is the cosmic animator, and I find it illogical to say He entered into creation at a specific moment in history when all of creation is part of Him.

VI

2017

72

DO UNBELIEVERS 'SUPPRESS THE TRUTH'?

6th January 2017

"For the wrath of God is revealed from heaven against all ungodliness and unrighteousness of men, who suppress the truth in unrighteousness" (Romans 1:18 NKJV)

Reading this verse in Paul's letter to the Romans and the surrounding context raises a question in my mind that I would like to briefly discuss. Is everyone who doesn't believe in Jesus and the Gospel suppressing the truth?

I used to be an atheist, and the idea of God seemed silly to me, and even angered me. I thought that such belief was irrational and illogical. Saying that God exists seemed to be like saying fairies or unicorns exist, it was just crazy.

Was I suppressing the truth? I don't feel I was because in all truth I hadn't received a revelation of the reality of God. He was no more than a concept. I believe that we come to know about God's existence when by His grace He chooses to reveal Himself. This is the only way we can believe.

> *For by grace you have been saved through faith, and that not of yourselves; it is the gift of God* (Ephesians 2:8 NKJV)

It is perhaps a different thing to *know* God exists (because you have received a revelation) and still suppress the truth. That would be like lying to yourself. I don't believe the majority of unbelievers are suppressing the truth in this way. It's just that they are yet to receive a revelation of who God is. Surely, God is in control, and it is He who decides who knows Him.

❧ 73 ❧

LIFE'S TOO SHORT?

11th January 2017

"Life's too short". It's a saying that we've all heard countless times. The meaning behind the phrase is normally that we need to enjoy ourselves now because our life here on earth will soon be over. The phrase is decidedly secular and often accompanies destructive tendencies such as lusts and materialistic pleasures. Should I buy another pack of cigarettes? Yeah, life's too short! Should I buy that car I've been thinking about getting on credit? Oh go on then, life's too short! Should I hook up with that girl I like even though she's married? And so on...

But I want to flip this saying on its head and say in retaliation; eternity is *very* long! Yes I'm being a spoilsport, and if you could know the life I lived before I became a Christian you might argue that I have no right to preach about this. But coming to know Jesus as He is revealed in the Holy Scriptures has transformed the way I think about our life on earth, and crucially, our life after death.

Our Lord said we should strive to "Enter through the narrow gate. For wide is the gate and broad is the road that leads to destruction, and many enter through it." (Matthew 7:13) This is a stark warning, and when I read this scripture it gives me a kick up the backside in terms of my spiritual life, and leads me to ask: What must I do in this life to prepare for the infinitely longer life after death?

I don't think there's a straightforward answer to this question, but I believe all we need to know is contained within the pages of Scripture. The Holy Bible is God's revelation concerning all that's important for us to know in order to live a godly life. And I have found that the more I study Scripture and come to understand my life in context, the more I find fulfilment in my relationship with God, and the less I feel the tendency to make destructive decisions with the justification that life's too short.

If we can nurture an attitude that keeps eternity in mind we will live more happily and soberly during our earthly lives and also prepare for the infinitely longer life to come. Why not make this year the year you focus on what's truly important and open your mind to the God of the universe who is standing at the door to your heart and knocking?

MY FAVOURITE QUATRAINS

20th February 2017

I have a particular love for quatrains. I think they appeal to my perfectionist nature because they hold a kind of perfectly formed beauty. If you're not familiar with the term 'quatrain' it simply means a four line stanza in a poem.

Each of the four quatrains below contains something moving and profound and wonderful. I hope that you will enjoy these precious little gems as much as I do. They are perfect tweet material owing to their concise nature so if you like them feel free to share the love!

1. This one is currently pinned to my profile on Twitter and I think it's my favourite. The gospel in a single quatrain.

Because the sinless Saviour died

My sinful soul is counted free
For God the just is satisfied
To look on Him and pardon me.

2. I picked this one up a few years ago. I believe I discovered it in a book of prayers that my father gave me. Apparently it's engraved as an epitaph on a tombstone in the graveyard at Elgin Cathedral. I think it captures something truly wonderful about the God-fearing Christian begging for mercy from an almighty God.

Here lies Martin Elginbrod,
Hae mercy on my soul Lord God,
As I would do were I Lord God
And ye were Martin Elginbrod.

3. Next is the perfect quatrain to text to your friends on Easter Sunday, the day we celebrate Christ rising from the dead. I don't need to say much, this quatrain speaks for itself.

Tomb thou shalt not hold Him longer
Death is strong but life is stronger
Stronger than the dark, the light,
Stronger than the wrong, the right.

4. Finally, a beautiful quatrain that I discovered only this morning as I was reading a sermon from the Reformed Baptist preacher Charles Spurgeon. I don't know whether or not Spurgeon wrote it. The last line is a quote from the Bible (Deuteronomy 33:25). Text this one to a friend if they're going through a tough time.

Days of trial, days of grief,
In succession thou may'st see;
This is still thy sweet relief,
'As thy days, thy strength shall be.'

✳ 75 ✴

LIVING THE GOSPEL

24th February 2017

It's frightening. Approaching people on the street, praying for people we don't know, casting out demons, fighting spiritual battles. But this is what Jesus has called us to do. I believe that these activities encapsulate something of the true meaning of Matthew 16:24, where Jesus says, "Whoever wants to be my disciple must deny themselves and take up their cross and follow me."

Being a Christian is difficult. We have a certain peace, which comes from knowing that we are right with God. But we also have obstacles to overcome; we go through desert periods, we fast and abstain from many worldly pleasures, we suffer trials, and so on. Not only these things, but as 2 Timothy 3:12 states, "...all who desire to live a Godly life in Christ Jesus will be persecuted".

In recent weeks I've been learning a lot about how to live out my life as a true Christian, and God has been really challenging me. It started when I watched The Last Reformation movie on YouTube, after stumbling upon it by 'chance' one evening (nothing happens by chance). I will never be the same having seen that movie, which depicts a present day movement of people living out the kind of Christian life we find in the Bible in the Book of Acts.

After watching that movie and having been changed forever, I am now working through an online video course led by Torben Sondergaard, who by God's grace is leading the Last Reformation movement. The video training, called The Pioneer School, consists of 20 videos and I've watched the first five at the time of publishing this post. The message Torben communicates is simple and accessible, but also very powerful. The whole focus is on how to live in obedience to Christ's teaching as we find it in the Bible, rather than simply going to church every Sunday and leading an otherwise fairly secular life.

I would like to share some experiences from earlier today, when I took to the streets in the area where I live and asked God to give me the courage and boldness to speak to people and pray for people. I had been out yesterday with the same intentions, but due to fear hadn't approached anyone. By God's grace, today was very different.

As I left my flat I resolved that I would talk to the first person I encountered. So I introduced myself to a lady who was passing by, and asked her if she needed prayer for anything. She told me she was fine, but had a close friend with a chronic illness. I asked if I could pray for her friend and she said she was a Christian and that would be fine. As I prayed there on the street I could feel God moving. I have no way of knowing whether this person was healed or not, but I have faith that she was.

Several minutes later I saw the guy who lives in the flat next to me walking down the street. He would have walked past me as I was praying for the lady on the street. I asked him if he needed any prayer (we know each other a little but don't have much contact, I have invited him to church a few times but he hasn't joined me yet). He said he has had pain in his legs when walking. I laid a hand on his leg and said a short prayer, and he said the pain had gone! He then brought up the subject of church and said he would like to come with me some time soon.

The next people I spoke to were a couple of women, one older and one younger. I asked if they needed prayer for any physical or emotional pain. The younger lady said she was due to go for tests soon because she has been experiencing nausea and sickness, but doesn't have a diagnosis. She was very open and happy for me to pray, but I could feel the older lady was uncomfortable. I prayed for the younger lady, and asked her how she felt. She said she was feeling no sickness! I felt I wanted to pray for her more and find out more about her, but the older lady was becoming uncomfortable and impatient and wanted to walk away. I felt upset that I could not speak with and pray for these ladies more, and felt regret that I didn't persevere.

A few minutes later I walked past a train station and there was a guy sat on the railing playing with his phone. I told him I'm a Christian and asked him if he needed prayer for anything, but he adamantly said no, so I wished him well and carried on.

Walking through the park, there was a young man and woman who I presumed were a couple, and I introduced myself and asked them if they needed prayer. The man explained that they were brother and sister, and he said that they were having difficulties in their relationship with each other. It's so honest of him to admit that to me. I laid hands on them and prayed over their relationship and I felt God's presence. This was one of those prayers where I feel I was definitely in the right place at the right time, and although I cannot know for sure what will happen with them, I trust God to bring healing and restoration.

Next, I encountered a lady and her dog. The lady had a bright demeanour and was easy to talk to, so I imagined she might be a Christian, but she said she wasn't. We walked along together talking for a while, and she said she would appreciate prayer for her sisters, as there was strife in the family. We stopped and I prayed for her sisters, and then after we walked on I shared something of the gospel with her. She said she had a Bible but hadn't read it for a long time. I explained that the first time I read the New Testament it didn't really speak to me, but then years later, in different circumstances, it spoke to me in a powerful way. The lady said she was about to go on a Yoga retreat in America, and that she had been thinking about books to take with her and after our conversation she would think about taking a Bible. Praise God! I warned her about the deception I had experienced in the New Age spiritual movement, and shared with her from Scripture that the only way to the Father is through the Son, and that Jesus said "I am the way, the truth, and the life" (John 14:6).

I spoke to several other people who said they were fine and clearly didn't want to talk. There were two ladies with a pushchair who I encountered twice. The first time I spoke with them they were quite short with me and went on their way, and when I saw them again, I said hello and smiled, but they ignored me.

God told me to speak to one more person and then call it a day. So I was on my way back to my flat and a man was walking past. I introduced myself as a Christian, and before I could say anything else he replied, "I'm a pastor!". As he quickly shook my hand and walked off I said I was going to ask ask if he wanted healing and we both smiled and that was that! I love God's sense of humour.

I still have so much to learn about how to be a faithful disciple of Christ. I'm aware that God uses us in such a way that we grow, and although He always tests us, He never does so beyond our capacity to cope at any given time. Today was testing, but God was with me and He was merciful.

I'm so grateful to God for blessing me with all these interactions today, and I feel pleased that when I stand before the judgment seat of Christ one day I can look back on today and feel as though I was brave and really gave it a shot.

I will continue to watch Torben's online training and I am planning to meet up with other Christians to go out in a group to evangelise and heal the sick. There is so much power in Jesus' name, and He is alive and bringing healing and hope to people through His body of believers. I am hoping to use my new YouTube channel to share some of my experiences of walking the Christian walk in the coming months.

Being a disciple of Jesus does not mean simply going to church every Sunday. It means living in the way Jesus commanded in the Bible. It's tough, but Jesus said, "Heal the sick, raise the dead, cleanse those who have leprosy, drive out demons. Freely you have received; freely give." (Matthew 10:8) If you feel challenged by this calling, you're not alone. Rest assured, there are other believers who you can connect with who will help and encourage you as you go.

❦ 76 ❧

THE BIBLE AND HOMOSEXUALITY

7th April 2017

I'm aware that this is a topic that inflames opinions and passions. In order for me to explain my views it will be necessary to explain a bit about my background, and what has led me to believe the things I believe. I sincerely hope that you will stick with me to the end of the article and I hope it will be an interesting read.

Who Am I?

I'm a Christian, and have been following Jesus for about a decade. Before that I was very promiscuous spiritually and sexually.

As an atheist during my teenage years I had pretty much no regard for sexual morality. I wanted to have sex with beautiful women as much as possible. I was driven by lust and there was really nothing in my life that was inhibiting me from pursuing carnal pleasure at every opportunity. At university and then working in the music industry this kind of life seemed acceptable – there was no authority teaching me that my behaviour was destructive. Sex, drugs, and rock and roll were my life.

When I was about 20 years old, after watching my parents' relationship fall apart and my mother suffer from an aggressive form of cancer that would ultimately take her life, I started to question everything. I wanted to find out about suffering, about sickness, about spirituality, and about truth. My search for enlightenment had begun.

I was drawn to the New Age movement, and spent my days meditating and listening to spiritual teachers like Deepak Chopra, Alan Watts, Eckhart Tolle, Ramana Maharshi, and Mooji, among others. At one time, I was drawn into a cult led by Ratu Bagus which involved a spiritual practice called 'shaking meditation' which ultimately left me feeling wrecked and hopeless. I was obsessed with Eastern religion and the 'gurus' who claimed to hold the key to enlightenment or self-realisation. I put my trust in these figures, believing that by following them I would find the peace of mind I desperately craved.

My mental health deteriorated and I started to experience psychosis. For years I was living in a state of confusion, a kind of dream world which eventually led to me acting strangely and crossing the boundaries of socially acceptable behaviour. I experienced panic attacks, deep depression, delusions, aggression, and I tried to kill myself, although I was so confused at the time that I wasn't even aware of what I was doing.

You won't be surprised to learn that I ended up in hospital. Not from the suicide attempt, but after a serious episode of psychosis that led to me attack my housemate and then sleep rough in South London for a few days. I was sectioned and taken to a psychiatric ward. This was in 2007.

During that first spell in psychiatric hospital, I asked a member of staff for a Bible. Even to this day I am still not sure what prompted me to do this, and judging by my experience as an atheist and adherent to New Age spirituality, it was a strange thing to do. But when I began to read passages of Scripture in my hospital room it was as though God was talking into my life circumstances and I was experiencing the reality of God and learning about His character for the first time.

Why Care What the Bible Says?

In order for us to truly believe in God, we need to experience some kind of revelation. For me this came through my experience of psychosis, which was very spiritual, and also from reading the Bible. For many people, God is an empty idea that frustrates or even angers them, and I used to be that way myself. During my youth it seemed so irrational to me that there could be a God, because the veil had not been lifted, and the revelation had not yet come. It seemed as though there was no difference between believing in God and believing in fairies or 'flying spaghetti monsters' (to quote a phrase Richard Dawkins uses to ridicule believers).

But the Bible says, "...seek and you will find; knock and the door will be opened to you." (Matthew 7:7) I was certainly seeking with my whole heart, and I believe that often when we are truly broken – after searching everywhere for truth and only finding heartbreak – that is the moment when God reveals Himself. This is what happened in my case.

Since that spell in hospital in 2007, the Lord has been with me and has never left me. I didn't stop experiencing turbulent mental health, and I have questioned various aspects of the Christian faith, but through it all I experienced the peace and love of Jesus. The gospel made sense to me for the first time, and I began to enjoy a personal relationship with God, which is something that can't be explained, only experienced.

The Bible is different to all other books. It is God's chosen way of revealing Himself to humanity. We find within the pages of Scripture everything that we need to know in order to live a godly life. The Holy Spirit gave me a solid conviction that the Bible is infallible and inerrant, which I take to mean it is exactly as God intended it to be for the purposes He had and has in mind.

With God and the Bible firmly established at the centre of my life, I became a different person. When we fear God, our approach to moral issues changes. We choose to seek God's will in all matters, accepting His authority with humility, and trusting that He knows best. I put an end to sexual immorality after reading in Scripture that it displeases God.

If you are struggling with issues to do with sexuality and morality, I believe you will find the answers if you truly humble yourself and seek God's will. Let's look at a few passages from the Bible that are relevant to the subject of homosexuality, and then you can choose whether you want to obey God, or go your own way.

Old Testament:

Leviticus 18:22 NLT:

"**Do not practice homosexuality**, having sex with another man as with a woman. It is a detestable sin."

Leviticus 20:13 NLT:

"**If a man practices homosexuality**, having sex with another man as with a woman, both men have committed a detestable act…"

New Testament:

1 Corinthians 6:9-10 NLT:

"Don't you realize that those who do wrong will not inherit the Kingdom of God? Don't fool yourselves. Those who indulge in sexual sin, or who worship idols, or commit adultery, or are male prostitutes, **or practice homosexuality**, or are thieves, or are greedy people, or drunkards, or are abusive, or cheat people – none of these will inherit the Kingdom of God."

Conclusion

I believe the above scriptures make it pretty clear how God views homosexuality. But there is good news. Jesus came to bring the gospel to sinners who are willing to repent and turn towards God and receive forgiveness. If you practice homosexuality, you have an opportunity to turn to God and receive forgiveness because of the sacrifice of Jesus Christ on the cross.

We are all sinners, so you have no reason to believe you are being singled out or judged more harshly than anyone else. I admit that I am a sinner in need of forgiveness, and I want to live God's way, not my own way. That means making sacrifices and giving up things that displease God. I would encourage you to accept God's free gift of grace today. Turn to Him and receive all that Jesus has done for you.

"If you confess with your mouth that Jesus is Lord and believe in your heart that God raised him from the dead, you will be saved." (Romans 10:9)

MY HOLY SPIRIT BAPTISM

17th April 2017

I'm going through a season of growth at the moment and have been asking God to reveal those things that I lack spiritually when it comes to salvation and embracing everything He has for me in Christ. I've been a little confused in the area of Holy Spirit baptism, because although I often feel 'filled with the Spirit', especially during worship, until today there hadn't been a significant event I could recall where I could say I experienced Holy Spirit baptism.

I sent text messages to several friends yesterday asking if they had been baptised by the Holy Spirit and "Yes!" "Wow!" "It's amazing!" were the kind of responses I got. So I felt more confused because I couldn't recall such an event from my own walk as a Christian. I was back at that familiar place that has arisen many times during my spiritual journey where I find myself asking, 'What am I missing?'

I met my friend Nick (not his real name) in a cafe today and we talked about many things to do with our spiritual walks and what God is doing in our lives. Nick and I had been texting about the specific issue of the Holy Spirit, and we got our Bibles out and looked at a few scriptures that were relevant to Holy Spirit baptism. I knew Nick had some experience of this as he has attended various seminars as part of the Last Reformation movement (see below).

It felt as though our conversations were leading somewhere, and after a while I suggested we go for a walk and we agreed that we would find a quiet area and then Nick would pray for me to be filled with the Holy Spirit. We made our way through busy central London to Russell Square, and found a quiet grassy area where we could pray.

I felt hopeful about what I might experience but I can't say I had 100% confidence I was going to experience anything. This is partly because I considered that to a certain extent I already "had" the Holy Spirit, and partly because I didn't know whether God would choose to work through Nick in order to give me a new experience.

As Nick began to pray, for the first few seconds I felt nothing, but then *WHAM* it was as though an aeroplane had flown directly over my head, I felt a wave of what could perhaps be described as fire passing through me and suddenly everything was clearer and there was peace. I wasn't expecting that! It happened as Nick was praying for the Holy Spirit to 'fill me up' – I did feel filled up and wanted him to keep praying because it was an amazing feeling!

We paused for a moment to discuss what was going on and were both delighted that I had experienced something. We agreed to continue praying. Nick was intermittently speaking in tongues and urged me to open my mouth and start speaking in tongues, which I did, and it felt strong and powerful and natural. I didn't want this experience to stop and wished that Nick had continued asking the Spirit to 'fill me up' more and more, but he started praying about other things and the power halted. What can I say, Nick isn't very experienced with this so it was a learning experience for both of us!

After a few minutes we stopped praying and started walking and talking about what had happened. I said I was so grateful to God that He had given me this experience, and I felt that now I could relate to my friends who had had similar experiences. It felt like an important step on my spiritual journey.

There is so much still to learn. In the coming months, I hope to continue to grow as a Christian, learning more about what true Biblical discipleship means and living the authentic Christian life. If you resonate with this ambition and haven't yet seen the Last Reformation movie, it is essential viewing, it changed my life and I can't recommend it strongly enough!

❧ 78 ❧

TIME IS SHORT

20th July 2017

I'm grateful to God for all He has done to unfold my life with such care, attention, discipline, adventure, and love. I turned 35 this week and I'm aware that I've now spent more time on Earth than Jesus did during His incarnation. That's quite a thought, that all the richness of my Saviour's life and ministry was completed in so short a span of time.

As Solomon says in the book of Ecclesiastes:

> *Life is fleeting, like a passing mist.*
> *It is like trying to catch hold of a breath;*
> *All vanishes like a vapor; everything is great vanity.* (Ecclesiastes 1:2)

Our stay on Earth is brief. Do we really have time to delay focusing on our spiritual situation? If we are aware that there is an afterlife, shouldn't we be compelled to seek after truth wherever it may be found, even if it means making a concerted effort to prioritise matters of faith in the midst of our busy schedules?

Jesus is calling to us from the pages of Scripture, giving us tender promises, telling us that He will carry our burdens. And if we believe that God raised Jesus from the dead and that Jesus is Lord, we can receive the most precious gifts this mortal life has to offer; the forgiveness of our sins and the hope of eternal life.

Friends, I don't know how long the Lord will extend my days, but that is not something I worry about. Whether I live a long time or just a little longer is a matter of little consequence, so long as I am accepted by God and in right relationship with Him. Having repented and received the precious Christian gifts of baptism in water and the Holy Spirit, I feel (in my more confident moments) that I am forgiven and accepted by God.

Admittedly, I do fear God and the day of judgement, for God is awesome in power and I am still sometimes haunted by my past sin. But I hold fast to the promise of Romans 8:1: "There is now no condemnation to those who are in Christ Jesus, who do not walk according to the flesh, but according to the Spirit."

Spurred on by such a hope, I can thank God in faith for the salvation He has promised, and sing with delight the words of the classic gospel song, 'Angel Band':

My latest sun is sinking fast,

My race is nearly run
My strongest trials now are past,
My triumph has begun
Oh, come angel band
Come and around me stand
Oh, bear me away on your snow white wings
To my immortal home
Oh, bear my longing heart to him
Who bled and died for me
Whose blood now cleanses from all sin
And gives me victory

Jesus is simply too important not to be taken seriously, so wherever you are at in your spiritual journey, get to know the Son of God while you still have time.

79

TWO-DAY ADVENTURE WITH GOD

7th August 2017

This weekend my friend Nick and I drove to Yeovil, which is a town in Somerset in the south west of England. We were attending a kickstart seminar, which is a Christian discipleship and evangelism event. I had seen many videos from events like this online through my interest in the Last Reformation movement, but this would be the first time I had attended one of these events.

The first couple of hours of the event, on Saturday morning, were a bit nervy for me as I was meeting so many people for the first time and was in unfamiliar circumstances. I was, however, trusting that God wanted me to be there, and would bless the occasion. I have heard people referring to the Last Reformation movement as a cult, and I have had unpleasant experiences with cults in the past, so mixed in with my faith in God was a little trepidation.

About 30 people were attending the event, and it was obvious from the outset that despite our diverse personalities and backgrounds we shared a love of God and a passion for the gospel and for following Jesus in an authentic, Biblical way. The morning sessions consisted of teaching about stepping out in faith, the gospel, and how to pray for people who needed healing. We had some lunch and then split up into 'teams' to go out on the streets of Yeovil and pray for people who were willing to let us do so.

Within a few minutes of approaching people on the street, my teammate Michael and I witnessed a powerful miracle. There was a gentleman with two crutches who said he had pain throughout his body. We laid hands on him and Michael commanded the pain to go in the name of Jesus, and after only two prayers the man was astonished that all his pain left completely. This was the first time I had witnessed such a powerful healing, and we praised God for His goodness. The man said he would consider coming to the kickstart event the following day (he didn't come as far as I'm aware but he still had a life-changing God encounter and saw Jesus in action).

A few minutes later we approached a couple of guys on a bench, one with a hat and a bright t-shirt whose name was Sunny D. He said he had pain in his lower back and that we could pray for him. I said one or two short prayers and he was amazed that the pain completely left. Seeing these healings was amazing for me too, as when I have prayed for people in the past I haven't always been confident that they were healed completely, only partially. Either that or they didn't want to admit they were healed due to being atheists or peer pressure or some other reason.

A little later we approached a group of young people who seemed to be into alternative culture, with their tattoos and piercings and dark clothing. Some were a little hesitant to talk to us but we found a man who was in serious pain and was due to go into hospital for a back operation soon following a car accident. We prayed for this guy many times and he said there was an improvement, but some of the others with him were resisting what we were doing through fear or scepticism or whatever and eventually a girl in the group led the others to move on.

Over the next few hours we spoke to dozens of people, sometimes praying, sometimes sharing the gospel, and many people were very open. We did have some rejections, but that is to be expected when you step out and approach people in this way. I could tell many testimonies about the people we met and the conversations we had, but let me just say that it was a wonderful few hours and I believe God used us to change many people's lives.

Back at base in the afternoon we shared testimonies, and it was great to hear the stories of other people from the kick-start. Some people who our teams had met on the street had given their lives to Christ and been healed and encouraged. I truly believe that by God's grace we had a significant impact on the town of Yeovil and it's amazing what can be accomplished in a few hours of dedicated evangelism.

After the testimonies we sang some worship songs, and it was so joyful. Just to be able to thank and praise God for what he has done for us in Jesus, and for what he was doing in Yeovil. I felt real freedom to sing out to God from my heart and the worship was so powerful that it brought my friend to tears. We are not ashamed of the gospel, for it is the power of God unto salvation for all who believe! (Romans 1:16)

Sunday was also a wonderful day, but in a different way. There was more teaching and some people headed out on the streets again but I spent much of the day immersed in conversation with my Christian brothers and sisters in the hall where we were gathered. I was really touched by the dedication of these people to their faith, and I had many great chats and forged some exciting new connections. Some people were baptised (praise the Lord!) which I was hoping to be a part of, but there was so much going on in the various different rooms that I missed the baptisms.

It's important to point out that as Christians we are always growing and seeking to love one other in deeper and more Christlike ways. Because we are imperfect, we sometimes struggle. Some of the conversations I had were really difficult. People were going through tough times, and I have my own insecurities and frailties which always surface more when I'm in a group of people. I have a spiritual sensitivity which means I can get overwhelmed easily, and this can be a real challenge.

I feel as though I am mature in some aspects of my spiritual walk, but in other aspects I am still broken and need healing. I try to remember that life is a journey, and as believers with the Holy Spirit living in us we have a joy and a victory, but we are also still broken and struggling due to our human nature. There were people in the group who didn't get healed, who were very upset, and struggling in many ways. This is also part of being a human being and being a Christian as we are not perfect like Jesus.

God blessed our drive back home to London on Sunday evening and I'm so happy to write this article to reflect on what was an awesome weekend, and an amazing two-day adventure with God.

❦ 80 ❧

CAN I LOSE MY SALVATION?

14th August 2017

Over on the Facebook group I set up to accompany my YouTube Channel, we've been having a discussion about whether or not it is possible for a Christian to lose their salvation. This question has been hotly debated by theologians. The idea that we cannot lose our salvation is sometimes referred to as 'the doctrine of eternal security' or 'the perseverance of the saints'.

In this post, I will present some of the key scriptures on both sides of the argument, with a little commentary, and then I will state my conclusions at the end. The discussion will not be exhaustive, but I will recommend a couple of books for further reading on this subject as I conclude.

Scriptures that Support Eternal Security

"I give them eternal life, and they shall never perish; no one can snatch them out of my hand. My Father, who has given them to me, is greater than all, no one can snatch them out of my Father's hand" (John 10:28-29b)

The promise of eternal life for believers is spoken about often in the New Testament (e.g. John 3:16, 1 John 5:13, Romans 6:23, etc). Those who support the doctrine of eternal security argue that if we can lose our salvation, then the life that we receive in Christ is not eternal, which would render all of these scriptures redundant. If no one can snatch believers out of Jesus' hand, that would seem to imply that the gift of eternal life is permanent.

"Now to Him who is able to keep you from stumbling, and to present you faultless before the presence of His glory with exceeding joy"
(Jude 24)

The phrase 'to keep you from stumbling' is rendered as 'to keep you from falling away' in the NLT version. This scripture seems to suggest that once we are saved, we are in God's hands, and if God has the power to save us He also has the power to keep us.

"And do not grieve the Holy Spirit of God, by whom you were sealed for the day of redemption." (Ephesians 4:30)

Baptism in the Holy Spirit is often talked about as a seal that means we have entered into right relationship with God (e.g. Ephesians 1:13). If receiving the Holy Spirit in this way is a seal, then it wouldn't necessarily make sense that the seal can be broken. For if we can lose our salvation, doesn't this render the seal somewhat meaningless?

> *"For I am persuaded that neither death nor life, nor angels nor principalities nor powers, nor things present nor things to come, nor height nor depth, nor any other created thing, shall be able to separate us from the love of God which is in Christ Jesus our Lord."* (Romans 8:38-39)

This might seem like a knock-down argument in favour of the case of eternal security. If *nothing* can separate us from God's love, doesn't this mean it is impossible for us to fall away once we have been saved?

Scriptures that Question Eternal Security

> *"Now the works of the flesh are evident, which are: adultery, fornication, uncleanness, lewdness, idolatry, sorcery, hatred, contentions, jealousies, outbursts of wrath, selfish ambitions, dissensions, heresies, envy, murders, drunkenness, revelries, and the like; of which I tell you beforehand, just as I also told you in time past, that those who practice such things will not inherit the kingdom of God."* (Galatians 5:19-21)

This scripture presents a stark warning that if we practice sin we may compromise our entry into the Kingdom of God. 'Inheritence' is a word that in this context may refer to salvation or attaining a place in heaven.

> *"For if, after they have escaped the pollutions of the world*

through the knowledge of the Lord and Savior Jesus Christ, they are again entangled in them and overcome, the latter end is worse for them than the beginning. For it would have been better for them not to have known the way of righteousness, than having known it, to turn from the holy commandment delivered to them. But it has happened to them according to the true proverb: 'A dog returns to his own vomit,' and, 'a sow, having washed, to her wallowing in the mire.'" (2 Peter 2:20-22)

This passage appears to suggest that if after coming to Christ we return to a life of sin we are committing a terrible evil. This passage strikes fear into the heart of the Christian as so many of us have had engaged in sinful activities after we have come to know Christ. Is this scripture suggesting that a return to such sin forfeits our salvation?

"...if you want to enter into life, keep the commandments." (Matthew 19:17)

These words of Jesus to the rich young ruler could be taken to suggest that we cannot enter the Kingdom of God if we break the commandments.

"Therefore, my beloved, as you have always obeyed, not as in my presence only, but now much more in my absence, work out your own salvation with fear and trembling; for it is God who works in you both to will and to do for His good pleasure." (Philippians 2:12-13)

Paul's use of the phrase 'work out your salvation' is our central concern here. If salvation is a process, as this verse suggests, to many this implies that we must act in the right way in order to be saved, so continually living in sin could perhaps compromise our right standing with God.

Conclusion

In my studies on this matter I have carefully considered all of the key scriptures that relate to the subject of eternal security, and I have presented many of those scriptures in this article. I feel the weight of evidence points to the idea that once we are truly saved, we cannot lose our salvation. There are many passages in Scripture that warn Christians against sinning, because sinning displeases God. God doesn't want us to sin, but I believe once we are saved we are given a new heart (Ezekiel 36:26), so if we are truly saved, God will give us the strength to persevere and keep His commandments. If we do slip up and need to repent, we have the hope that God will forgive us, for Jesus' sake.

I believe the core question at the heart of this debate is 'Who saves, God, or man?'. If man is responsible for his salvation then it would make sense that we can fall away because we are free to choose evil actions at any point. But if Almighty God is in control of our lives, as I believe He is, then He is perfectly capable of saving us with certainty and finality.

I don't believe God has any obligation to keep us eternally secure; but rather it is a gift that He has promised in Scripture for those who believe. God is always true to His Word. Jesus Himself said the Scriptures cannot be broken (John 10:35). So this should give us confidence that if we believe in

Jesus, and have repented and been baptised in His name, we will be saved.

> *"All that the Father gives me will come to me, and whoever comes to me I will never cast out... No one can come to me unless the Father who sent me draws him. And I will raise him up on the last day."* (John 6:37,44)

> *My Father, who has given them to me, is greater than all, and no one is able to snatch them out of the Father's hand.* (John 10:29)

✣ 81 ✣

SOME TRUTHS ABOUT GOD

25th August 2017

There is only one God, who is omnipresent and therefore all that exists. The entirety of creation is God's self-expression, and there is nothing that exists that is not part of God. Every created thing is sustained by God, and under His direct control. All creatures are like puppets in the metaphorical hands of God.

God has existed eternally; He never had a beginning and will never have an end. His essence is beyond definition, but He is not a material object like a human being, He is pure being or spirit. God is living in this single eternal moment – existence and God are not ontologically different from one another.

God is self-sufficient, independent, and autonomous.

God is capable of producing in human beings a mode of mind that is like a veil – it can prevent us from being aware of Him.

He is also able to reveal Himself to the human mind by speaking directly to it in a mode similar to but distinct from contemplative thought. It is God who makes thoughts arise in our minds, both contemplative thoughts and those thoughts that are His speech to us. We can experience thoughts that are ours, and others that are God's. They are similar, but distinct, and all are from God.

As well as speaking to us directly, God also reveals Himself in visions, dreams, and Scriptures. For those to whom God has granted insight, the wonder and harmony of creation is further evidence of His existence and His nature.

God is the creator of every object, the author of every book, the composer of every song. We can observe that He is able to create billions of distinct objects and creatures, and so we say He is infinite in His creative powers.

God has created every belief and every religion. Every idea is an expression from God. All that humans call good, and all that they call evil, are from God. It is impossible for anything to happen that is not the will of God, so we do not have free will.

❧ 82 ❧

THE FLEXIBILITY OF GOD

1st September 2017

In my studies in recent years I've focused a great deal of energy and attention on trying to understand the nature of God. This is not a purely intellectual pursuit, as the way we see God has huge implications in terms of how we view different religions, and their doctrines. Our view of God affects the way we understand salvation, predestination, sin, judgment, and many other important subjects.

In my writing (both on my blog and in my books) I have presented arguments that point to God's sovereignty over all events, owing to the attribute of 'omnipresence' that I believe God has. If God is everywhere, then it follows that He is making all events and activity happen.

But the point I want to make in this brief post is that there is a certain *flexibility* in the will of God. God is a *living* God. He did not set the universe in motion, and then recline back on His throne in heaven and watch while everything unfolds in a mechanical fashion, as deists or determinists might argue. There is not separation between God and creation in this way, but instead God's presence pervades every part of the universe, and there is no place in existence where God is not.

In the book of Psalms, we read: "Whatever the Lord pleases He does, in heaven and in earth, in the seas and in all deep places." (Psalm 135:6) This scripture depicts an *active* God who is present everywhere. Also, in the Book of Acts, Paul says, speaking of God, "For in Him we live and move and have our being" (Acts 17:28). This scripture depicts the kind of *panentheistic* God I believe in; a God who is greater than His creation but all of His creation exists within Him.

In *Unlocking the Bible* by David Pawson, which I'm currently reading, there is a quote which stood out and prompted me to write this post. Here's what Pawson says:

> *"There's a flexibility in God's sovereignty that we really must hold very precious, lest we slip in to the idea that God has predetermined everything, and we do not matter." (p 647)*

I love Pawson's use of the word 'flexibility'. If God is living, and omnipresent, then in every moment He has the power to choose how He unfolds the story of creation.

Now it may be the case, as Christians would argue, that God has a plan for His creation, which He has revealed in Scripture. I am not denying that God can make plans. What I am arguing is that there is nothing to stop God from choosing to unfold His creation in any way He chooses. God may make plans for the future, but they are not determined until He brings them about. This is the *flexibility* of God, and if you think about it, it's a wonderful thing.

✿ 83 ✿

IS EVERYTHING SUBJECTIVE?

4th September 2017

When I was studying for my undergraduate degree, I wrote my final year dissertation on the subjectivity of musical meaning. My argument was that the meaning of a piece of music is encapsulated not so much in the sounds we hear, but in the context in which we listen. My argument located musical meaning in the mind of the listener, rather than in the sound of the music.

While I was writing about this, I began to consider subjectivity in other areas of life, and started to doubt there was any such thing as objective truth. Surely, I thought, *everything* is subjective. Even in the domain of science, where objectivity defines a way of thinking, I started to see that it was scientific minds that formulated truth, rather than there being any kind of objective reality.

It's been a while since I've considered these things deeply, and no doubt my worldview has changed since I began to believe in God and study theology. If I reread my dissertation today it's likely that I would cringe at certain statements I made concerning the absolute subjectivity of all things. Having said that, I do believe I was making an important point, and I read a quote today that is just the kind of thing I would have written during my time at university:

> *You cannot write history without betraying your personal interest, because, from all that happens, you select the things that you are interested in and that you think are important.*

('Unlocking the Bible' by David Pawson, p703)

As with music, and perhaps science, history has a strong subjective element, and from a theological perspective we could say that the Biblical authors were biased by their cultural background and circumstances.

On the other hand, it could be argued that due to the inspired nature of Scripture (see 2 Peter 1:21), the Bible is a rare example of how objective truth does exist. In this context, there is a relationship between objectivity and *authority* (we see this in the truth claims of scientists as well) – for if everything in Scripture is open to infinite interpretations, this detracts from the force of any argument in favour of the Bible's infallibility and inerrancy.

With this in mind, I'll close with the following thought (which I expand upon in my books) and this is something for advocates of sola scriptura to consider:

Truth is not encapsulated in the markings on a page, but is the result of God working in the minds of human beings as they read.

Wouldn't you agree?

❧ 84 ❧

MAKING PLANS

12th September 2017

Nothing is definite. Everything in transient. God is in control of every aspect of our lives, and yet we are forced to live with uncertainty. The Bible tells us that God knows even the number of hairs on our heads; that's how close He is. He is behind every heartbeat and every thought and emotion.

We can be certain of God's existence, and of His intimate involvement in our lives, yet the truth is that God can alter the trajectory of our lives at any moment. How do we deal with this reality?

While our perspective is limited and veiled, God sees the bigger picture. Our problems may seem gigantic and painful and insurmountable, but to God there is a universe of infinite possibilities, and because He is in control, we are able to believe He can deliver us from the circumstances that trouble our minds, bodies, and spirits.

It is a great blessing to be aware that God exists. When God reveals Himself and begins to speak into our lives, our perspective shifts, and we live out each day focused on Him and in dependence on Him. The New Testament writer of the book of James knew this only too well:

> *Come now, you who say, "Today or tomorrow we will go to such and such a city, spend a year there, buy and sell, and make a profit";* [14] *whereas you do not know what will happen tomorrow. For what is your life? It is even a vapor that appears for a little time and then vanishes away.* [15] *Instead you ought to say, "If the Lord wills, we shall live and do this or that."* [16] *But now you boast in your arrogance. All such boasting is evil.* (James 4:13-16)

I do not see in the above scripture any instruction against thinking about the future, but rather a note of caution. Things might not turn out as you expect. As the proverb goes: When we make plans, God laughs.

So, in respect of this, knowing God is a double-edged sword. We gain security from the knowledge that God is in control, but we never know what each day will bring, which can be frightening and unsettling. I think all of this can be summed up in a single word which points us to the essential ingredient in this mysterious existence. That word is 'faith', and in a greater or lesser measure, we all must have it.

JESUS AS LOGOS

28th September 2017

The writer of the book of John opens his gospel with some very well-known words. These words have been used by theologians as evidence that Jesus has existed eternally, along-side God the Father and God the Holy Spirit:

> *In the beginning was the Word, and the Word was with God,*
> *and the Word was God. He was in the beginning with God.*
> *All things were made through Him, and without Him*
> *nothing was made that was made. In Him was life, and the*
> *life was the light of men. And the light shines in the darkness,*
> *and the darkness did not comprehend it.* (John 1:1-5 NKJV)

I have found this to be a difficult passage to fully comprehend, and I think many Christians would agree that it's some-what mysterious. When I think about Jesus, I picture in my mind a human form, and I'm not easily able to equate that human form with the 'Word' of John's Gospel. What exactly is this 'Word' that was with God in the beginning, and how can that Word possibly be the same thing as the embodied Christ who lived in human form?

I came across an interesting passage today in a book I'm reading which has helped me to understand this mystery a little more clearly. I will quote the passage below, and then make a few brief comments to round off the article. Please note that the word 'Logos' is the original Greek term that has been translated into our Bibles as 'Word' in John 1.

A little history will help explain why John chose to call Jesus the Logos. This concept had particular meaning in Ephesus, where John was writing. Six hundred years before there lived in Ephesus a man called Heraclitus, acknowledged as the founder of science. He believed in the necessity of scientific enquiry, probing the natural world, asking how and why things were the way they were. Was it merely chance? Were we in a chaotic universe or was there an order?

He looked for patterns or 'laws' to see if he could deduce some logic behind the operations of the natural world. He used the word 'logos' to stand for 'the reason why', the purpose behind what took place. When he looked at life (bios) he looked for the logos; when he studied the weather (meteor) he sought the logos. This concept now appears in our words for the study of different areas of science: biology, meteorology, geology, psychology, sociology, etc.

So Heraclitus said that the logos is 'the reason why'. Every branch of science is looking for the logos, the reason why things are as they are. John, realizing that Jesus is the ultimate reason 'why' everything happened, took up this idea and called Jesus the logos, 'the Word'. The whole universe was made for him. He was the Logos before there was anyone else to communicate with. That is the reason why we are here. It is all going to be summed up with him. He is the 'Reason Why'.

('Unlocking the Bible' by David Pawson, William Collins 2015, p 902)

It may be the case that it's impossible for human beings to envisage what an eternal Jesus looks like, but this passage certainly provides an explanation which makes the concept a little easier to understand. Pawson takes the focus off Jesus' embodied form, and onto what could be described as an abstract concept.

✣ 86 ✣

THE LOGOS AS A PERSON

29th September 2017

In my most recent article I looked at an interesting way of understanding what it means for the person of Jesus to have been the 'Word' or 'Logos' from eternity past, as is indicated in the opening of the Gospel according to John. Today, I want to expand upon the same topic, and will again be quoting David Pawson and his excellent Bible commentary.

We saw in yesterday's article that the word 'logos' can be translated as 'the reason why'. So in John's gospel, when the author says 'In the beginning was the Word [logos]' he was saying 'In the beginning was the reason why'. So Jesus is 'the reason why' God created the universe.

This turns the eternal Jesus into a kind of abstract concept. But Christians talk about Jesus as being an eternal *person*.

While seeing the eternal Jesus as 'the reason why' seems helpful and easy to understand, the phrase doesn't actually encapsulate the personhood of Christ.

So how are we to understand the personhood of Jesus prior to the Incarnation?

Let's see what Pawson has to say in respect of this problem:

> *The word [logos] has another phase in its history too, this time across the Mediterranean Sea from Ephesus in Alexandria, Egypt. Alexandria had a school which combined Greek and Hebrew thinking, in part because there were many dispersed Jews living in the city. This school, or university, was the location for the translation of the Old Testament into Greek by 70 scholars known as the 'Septuagint' or 'LXX'. One of the Jews involved was a professor called Philo. In seeking to interpret Hebrew thinking into Greek, Professor Philo seized on the word Logos and said that the Logos was not to be spoken of as 'it' but as 'he'. He was 'personifying' the Logos, rather in the way that in Proverbs wisdom is personified as a woman.*

('Unlocking the Bible' by David Pawson, William Collins 2015, p 903)

So we see from this snippet of history the origins of the personification of the logos. It seems that when Philo used the term 'he' to refer to the pre-incarnate Jesus, this is a figure of speech, rather than pointing to a physical embodied person. The analogy of wisdom personified in the book of

Hebrews is helpful, as surely wisdom in reality doesn't have a physical form.

So we might conclude that the pre-incarnate Jesus was a person, but only figuratively so.

87

THE STATE OF IT ALL

28th October 2017

Britain is broken. Individualism is now the unspoken religion of the masses. There is no fear of God; no love of neighbour. Instead, fearing sickness and death, our citizens ask "How much money can I earn in order to buy security?" And they bully their way to each new promotion, trampling down their neighbour in the process, because they see others doing the same, and have no values to guide their conduct.

Most of our emotions are now defined as mental illnesses, and are treated with pills that have little effect other than to harm the body, and confuse the mind. We have a medical system in chaos, but because we are conditioned to regard doctors as saints, few people speak out about the way capitalism has corrupted healthcare. Doing so would be unpatriotic.

We are a multicultural country now, and we are told to celebrate this. But in truth, we are all confused, lacking identity, and lacking community. We no longer know what it means to be proud of our country; to have a shared sense of purpose. So many voted for Brexit because they are angry about what our society has become.

Since the Second World War we have enjoyed great privilege and power, but secularism has crept in and gradually we have lost sight of the God who blessed us so richly. To an increasing number of people in British society, God is irrelevant or even offensive.

The coffee shop assistant, on his break, puts his foot up on the chair and plays the sound from his phone loudly. He can't keep his eyes open. He has had only two hours sleep, as he was out partying for most of the night. He is in no fit state to work. He has no sense that he is a servant; that his conduct matters. He doesn't value his work - it is just a means to an end. He is a broken soul, in broken Britain.

Reading the papers and checking social media, there are stories about the murder of babies and adults. Everyone is asserting their rights, even the right to kill their offspring, to change their gender, to put themselves first. There is no compassion, but instead, everyone is asking, 'What about me?' Every man for himself. Every woman for herself. This is broken Britain.

Families are fragmented and devoid of values. Relationships are about lust and sex rather than mission, humility, and service. So many are confused about gender and sexual orientation, and society's solution is to offer surgery and pills rather than love and care. Our children's role models are pop stars who are famous for fame's sake, not because they have something valuable to offer society.

Our Prime Minister, bereft of ideas, speaks of 'The British Dream'. It is a fantasy, there is no such thing; she is running on empty. Britain is broken, and I am so sad about the state of it all.

88

IS IT REALLY WORTH IT?

2nd November 2017

I wanted to write a short blog post about *fighting battles*. When life presents you with a circumstance where you feel you are being treated unfairly, is it wise to put up a fight, or is it better to absorb the frustration, let go, and move on?

Let's look at one area in particular: money. Money causes friction and is the battleground of capitalist culture; just look at the way lawyers, solicitors, estate agents, and bankers operate. We live in a world where people are constantly trying to acquire wealth, and are willing to take a bite out of each other in order to get the financial 'security' they crave.

I've noticed that there's a direct correlation between how rooted I am in my faith in God, and how I respond to situations where I feel someone is trying to take advantage of me. When I'm rooted in the teaching of Scripture, the need to 'fight back' evaporates, because my mind is centred on the One who is able to meet all my needs in ways I can't even imagine.

There is one scripture in particular that speaks volumes on this subject, and it can be found in Paul's first letter to the Corinthians:

> *"To have lawsuits at all with one another is already a defeat for you. Why not rather suffer wrong? Why not rather be defrauded?"*
> (1 Corinthians 6:7 ESV)

To most people in capitalist societies, this teaching is totally counter-intuitive. Our instinct is to put up a fight. But I believe fighting always shows a lack of faith in our Creator, who we must trust to fight our battles in the spiritual dimension, and who will judge those who have treated us unfairly.

❧ 89 ❧

CHRISTIAN LOVE

11th November 2017

I recently read a tweet from a Christian that touched me in a profound way:

> *We become more and more joyless and call it Jesus. More and more hateful and call it holiness. Less and less creative and call it maturity. We like fewer and fewer people and call it sanctification. We must think Jesus had the worst personality on earth.*

I believe that on the whole Christians are well-intentioned, and because Christians have a profound fear of God (and hell) they are desperate for others to know Jesus and practise sound doctrine. But I also recognise that if we're not careful, the fear of God can turn us into horrible people.

I have been guilty of rebuking people for what I have regarded as ungodly behaviour. When Christians do this we feel as though we are sticking up for the gospel and helping people. But let us always keep in mind what Jesus said about judging others:

> And why do you look at the speck in your brother's eye, but do not consider the plank in your own eye? Or how can you say to your brother, 'Let me remove the speck from your eye'; and look, a plank is in your own eye? Hypocrite! First remove the plank from your own eye, and then you will see clearly to remove the speck from your brother's eye. (Matthew 7:3-5 NKJV)

It seems to me that no two Christians believe exactly the same things. So we should be especially careful about rebuking one another, and aim instead to show love and kindness, care and understanding, and empathy, with our neighbours.

Surely the fruit of the Spirit, as we read about in Galatians, should be evident in the lives of believers if we are truly committed to living in a godly way:

> But the fruit of the Spirit is love, joy, peace, longsuffering, kindness, goodness, faithfulness, gentleness, self-control. (Galatians 5:22-23a NKJV)

Perhaps you have noticed yourself turning into a hard-hearted, joyless, uncreative, self-righteous Christian who is so eager not to be tainted by 'the world' that you find yourself living in a hateful bubble. If so, is it time to re-examine your faith and seek God afresh?

🦋 90 🦋

LORD OVER MY LIFE

17th November 2017

Lord over my life,

You are behind my every breath.

You know me more intimately

than I know myself.

With a troubled mind,

I cry out to you,

In a way familiar to all of those,

Who struggle with being human.

　　　　　　　　·　·　·

Lord, consider my predicament,

Search me and show me,

In what way do I err?

What must I do to once again

Feel your love, grace, and peace?

"As the heavens are higher than the earth, so are my ways higher than your ways and my thoughts than your thoughts." (Isaiah 55:9)

You have created a universe,

So expansive and complex,

That no man could ever fathom

Its workings.

You see smaller than the microscopes

And bigger than the telescopes

And all this with ease – such ease

That you can sustain a universe

For ten thousand years.

"Great is our Lord, and mighty in power; His understanding is infinite" (Psalm 147:5)

Lord, I'm so confused.

Moral decisions trouble me

Personalities trouble me

Circumstances trouble me

I am greatly grieved in my spirit

For I know not what I should do.

I feel an oppressive canopy

Over my mind

A ceiling that is solid

That you are holding in place.

It must be you, Lord,

Despite what others say,

For you have shown me,

You are in control of all things.

"Our God is in the heavens; He does all that He pleases." (Psalm 115:3)

Perhaps you have sent satan to test me,

As I know others will suggest,

But you have revealed to me, Lord,

That you have power over all things,

The forces of good, and the forces of evil.

"The LORD works out everything to its proper end − even the wicked for a day of disaster" (Proverbs 16:4)

Perhaps it is for my protection

And part of a much grander plan

That you oppress my spirit.

Yet in this moment it troubles me

I fear I am acting incorrectly

That your wrath may be lurking

That you might unleash uncertainty

Or calamity, or disease, or distress

On my weak and troubled soul.

Do not punish me, Lord,

For I cannot act outside your will.

Please be merciful Lord,

Do not punish your own handiwork.

I am angry at this world, Lord God,

But I beg of you,

Do not let me ever be angry with You.

Be my hope and my security,

Hear my crying, see my tears,

And comfort me.

Assure me once again,

That you love me,

That everything will be okay.

"And we know that all things work together for good to those who love God, to those who are called according to His purpose." (Romans 8:28)

Lord, send an Angel,

To encamp around me

And protect me

From anyone

Or anything

That would seek to rob me

Of Your peace.

Give me wisdom,

Give me guidance,

Give me assurance,

Be tender,

Be kind,

Be merciful.

"Call on Me in the day of trouble; I will deliver you, and you shall glorify Me." (Psalm 50:15)

Let it be so. Amen.

91

IS GOD ABLE TO LIE?

8th December 2017

It seems to me logical, sensible, and obvious, that an all-powerful God, who is creator and sustainer of the universe, can do whatever He pleases. Indeed, there is a scripture that says as much:

> *But our God is in heaven;*
> ***He does whatever He pleases.***
> (Psalm 115:3 NKJV)

Yet I often hear Christians saying that God cannot lie, and there does appear to be scriptural justification for this:

> *Thus God, determining to show more abundantly to the heirs*
> *of promise **the immutability of His counsel**,*
> *confirmed it by an oath, that by two immutable things, in*

*which **it is impossible for God to lie**, we might have strong consolation, who have fled for refuge to lay hold of the hope set before us.*
(Hebrews 6:17-18 NKJV)

I have quoted two scriptures from the Bible that could be seen to contradict one another, for surely either God isn't able to lie, or He can do whatever He pleases, but both statements can't be true. It's an important problem to consider, and readers may see this problem differently according to the degree to which they affirm the Bible to be inerrant and/or infallible.

Is there a way that both of the above quotations can be true? Or would you agree with me that to say God cannot lie places restrictions on His being; and we cannot restrict an omnipotent God?

92

TWO VITAL QUESTIONS

12th December 2017

I have read the whole Bible and attended various Catholic and Protestant churches, and after much study and exploration I believe I have a pretty good idea of the central doctrines and tenets of the Christian faith. Those who have read my essay entitled *An Almighty Predicament: A Discourse on the Arguments For and Against Christianity* will know that there are some aspects of Christian doctrine that I struggle to accept and believe.

I have come to realise that there are two questions that I need to find answers to in order to determine whether or not I should be a Christian.

1. Is Jesus the only way to have peace with God?

2. Is the Bible God's only revelation for people today in relation to spiritual Truth?

These two questions are interrelated. Jesus claims that He is the only way to the Father (John 14:6). But of course, we know about this claim from the Bible, so it only needs to be believed if the Bible represents absolute and exclusive Truth.

Within Christianity there are many different interpretations concerning what constitutes Truth. Learned Biblical scholars differ wildly concerning which interpretation of particular scriptures is correct, so it seems that interpretation is to a certain extent subjective. After all, the words of Scripture are merely markings on pages – the way we come to understand what is written is by God working in us as we read and reflect, and He can do this in myriad different ways.

The sole authority of the Bible is disputed by Catholics who believe Truth must be interpreted and defined by the leaders of the Catholic church. There are also many other groups who argue that the Protestant canon isn't the exclusive embodiment of Truth and that we can find truth in nature, reason, and logic, as well as in other Scriptures, whether it be the Qur'an, or the Book of Mormon, or some other supposedly inspired collection of writings.

How are we to know whether the 66 books of the Protestant Bible represent absolute and exclusive Truth? I believe the only way is through revelation from God to the human mind, resulting in a certain understanding or posture of faith. It must be a matter that we pray about, and ask God to help us discern.

Ultimately, what we believe to be true comes down to faith, and faith, I believe, comes from God. He is working out His plan for existence with sovereign authority, and whatever He wills us to believe is what we will believe. If you maintain it's possible for us to believe things that are contrary to God's will, then you are saying God is not in control of our lives, which is a belief that many Christians hold, but with which I profoundly disagree (read *An Almighty Predicament* for a detailed account of my reasons why).

In my understanding, God is completely sovereign, creation is His handiwork, and He is in control of all the details, including every aspect of our lives; our thoughts, words, actions, and beliefs (wouldn't it be strange to pray to a God who *isn't* in control?). And if I am to wholeheartedly dedicate my life to the teachings of Jesus Christ as we find them in the Bible, it will depend on God's guidance, revelation, and ultimately, His will.

So I pray:

Lord God, shape me into who You want me to be, guide me so that I know I am on the right path, help me to live in a way that pleases You always. Be merciful to me and save me from any thoughts, words or deeds that lead to destruction. Sovereign God, help me to have sound understanding in matters of theology and Truth, and eradicate from me anything that is false, unsound, or evil. Help me to live well and be a blessing to others, and to be a person who will always be held in Your favour. Even if it's difficult, Lord, show me the way. Amen.

VII
2018

PASCAL'S WAGER DISCUSSED

18th January 2018

Christianity might seem strange to some, particularly to those who haven't had a revelation of the reality of God. But when we come to understand the Christian worldview, and how it relates to every human being, we are all forced to consider seriously the idea of salvation and whether ignoring what the Bible says about life after death is really an option.

Such was the conclusion that 17th century French theologian Blaise Pascal arrived at, and which motivated him to compose what subsequently became known as Pascal's Wager.

Pascal's argument can be summarised as follows:

> 1. If you believe in God and God does exist, you will be rewarded with eternal life in heaven: thus an infinite gain.

2. If you do not believe in God and God does exist, you will be condemned to remain in hell forever: thus an infinite loss.

3. If you believe in God and God does not exist, you will not be rewarded: thus an insignificant loss.

4. If you do not believe in God and God does not exist, you will not be rewarded, but you have lived your own life: thus an insignificant gain.

The conclusion that can be drawn from the above statements is that when the odds are weighed, it is most rational to believe in God, and to live accordingly.

Problems with the Wager

There are several problems with the Wager that immediately come to mind. Firstly, the problem of different religions believing in different gods. Choosing to obey the Muslim god would lead to a completely different life than if one chose to obey the Christian god. Even if we agree with Pascal's argument, we are still faced with the question: Which god do I follow?

Alongside this problem there is also the fact that faith isn't a momentary decision, but rather a lifelong commitment. I would argue that even if one reaches the conclusion that the rational position is to believe in the Christian God, it's very difficult (perhaps impossible) to live a committed religious life, unless one's faith is genuine and springs from knowledge of God's existence rather than a mere intellectual decision.

The Possibility of Going to Hell

There's no doubt in my mind that the existence of hell is a logical possibility. I have experienced moments of horrible suffering in my life, and it's obvious to me that if God can make me suffer terribly in one moment, He could do so for eternity, if that were his will.

But would God really be so cruel? As I ponder my life experience, and the lives of others, I see that although people do suffer, and sometimes terribly, that suffering is always under control, and ultimately limited. It seems to me that God eventually liberates people from suffering, either by healing them, restoring their peace, or ending their lives. Of course, I have no idea what people experience in the afterlife, but I have a hope (and it can only be a hope) that God ultimately shows mercy to all sentient beings.

Divine Judgment and Free Will

The whole area of divine judgement is one I have considered deeply, and my personal view is that if God is in control of our lives, as I believe He is, then judgement is a peculiar concept. If there is a day of judgement, God will be judging His creatures for actions that have unfolded in accordance with His sovereign will, which seems strange. There is not space here to examine this problem in depth, but I have done so in my essay *An Almighty Predicament*, which looks at key arguments for and against Christianity.

Conclusion

While I feel the force of the argument presented in Pascal's Wager, I cannot be wholly dedicated to Christianity while there are certain areas of Christian doctrine that don't make logical sense to me. To suppress these areas is in my experience incredibly difficult, as whenever I am immersed in Christian living the doubts and problems I have with Christian doctrine come to the surface of my mind and make it virtually impossible to be wholly dedicated to the faith.

It's not a matter of backsliding, and I want to make that clear. It's not about falling into sin, or wanting to choose an easy life. I would rather lead a difficult life and avoid hell, of course. But I have a (God-given?) concern and passion for truth, and I find that however much I fear God, and fear hell, I am not able to come to terms with the inconsistencies in Christian doctrine that cause me to draw back from the faith.

❦ 94 ❦

MUST I LOVE MY ENEMIES?

5th February 2018

Envisage this scenario: You're a Christian and your next-door neighbour is keeping you awake playing oppressively loud music in the middle of the night every night despite your repeated attempts to ask him to let you sleep. You also hear him being abusive towards his son, and witness him dealing with every life circumstance with aggression and bullying.

He's been in prison several times for causing bodily harm to others, and you know he is currently engaged in criminal activity that has not been brought into the light. You and others are suffering a great deal as a result of this man's behaviour, and you feel that something needs to change, and quickly.

You know you need to pray for this guy, but what kind of prayer should you pray?

You reach for your Bible in the hope you can find some inspiration, and decide there must be something in the Psalms to
give you direction. You turn to Psalm 10, and read the
following passage, where David is crying out to God for
justice against his enemies:

> *For there is no faithfulness in their mouth;*
> *Their inward part is destruction;*
> *Their throat is an open tomb;*
> *They flatter with their tongue.*
> *Pronounce them guilty, O God!*
> *Let them fall by their own counsels;*
> *Cast them out in the multitude of their transgressions,*
> *For they have rebelled against You.*

(Psalm 5:9-10 NKJV)

That seems to fit your emotions perfectly! You are tempted to
get down on your knees and pray this prayer to God, asking
for your neighbour to be pronounced guilty and receive
punishment for his cruel behaviour.

But there is something holding you back. It doesn't feel quite
right to pray in that way, because you know Jesus said something important about loving your enemies. So you reach for
your Bible once more and turn to the book of Matthew:

> *"You have heard the law that says, 'Love your neighbour' and*
> *hate your enemy. But I say, love your enemies! Pray for those*
> *who persecute you!"* (Matthew 5:44)

All of a sudden you're conflicted. You need to pray over this situation with the guy next door, but do you pray for him to be arrested and face the justice of the legal system, or do you pray for God to change the guy's heart and forgive him – for mercy rather than justice?

My instinct tells me that Jesus is the ultimate authority, and so if we find ourselves in such a situation we should pray for a transformation of our neighbour's heart, and for God's grace and mercy in his life, rather than for him to be found guilty in the way that King David desired for his enemies and as expressed in the Psalms. After all, we have all done wicked things, and wouldn't we want God's mercy for our own transgressions?

CHRISTIAN MORALITY AND
ARTIFICIAL INTELLIGENCE

1st March 2018

The world in which we live today is so different in many ways to the world that the authors of the Christian Scriptures inhabited. This being so, Christians must continually reinterpret the moral lessons of the Bible so that we can heed their guidance in the 21st Century.

One area that presents a problem in this respect is our growing reliance on technology and artificial intelligence. The inventions of the digital age present us with scenarios that are unprecedented in human history, and pastors and theologians need to respond. In this short article, I will reflect a little on some of the new moral problems Christians will face in the coming years.

It may make Christians feel deeply uncomfortable, but it's likely that robots capable of sexual intercourse will be widely available before long. Some people might regard these as elaborate sex toys, but the question arises: If a married person engages in intercourse with a robot, have they committed adultery?

It would seem obvious to me that such an activity would be adulterous, but such a perspective is necessarily subjective as there is no guidance on this issue in the Bible. Perhaps the Catholic Church could score a few points here, as they could argue that the magisterium exists precisely to provide clarity on issues such as this where guidance is not explicitly found in Scripture.

This is one example of a wider issue which is that new inventions are increasingly blurring the line between what is biological and what is technological. We see this in the area of genetics and genome editing; one issue being whether or not it's morally acceptable to tamper with genes if such tampering will lead to the eradication of certain diseases, for instance.

In the coming years, every Christian is going to face difficult moral decisions concerning the extent to which they allow technology to infiltrate their biology. Electronic implants are already widely available for a variety of purposes, and it might not be long before we find ourselves under pressure to yield to invasive technologies that compromise those aspects of our lives where we currently enjoy biological freedom.

❧ 96 ❧

FROM MY HEART, TO GOD

13th March 2018

In all honesty, Lord, my main desire in life is to limit suffering as much as possible. I am most concerned with limiting my personal suffering, but I also care for all other sentient beings and don't want them to suffer either. You have given me a taste of suffering through mental breakdown, torture, depression, pain, and hopelessness. I am desperate not to experience terrible suffering in the future.

I believe You are in control of all suffering, and that any solution to the problem of suffering lies exclusively within Your power. You are clearly unfolding a plan for creation, and have shown me beyond any doubt that You are completely sovereign over my life, and all our lives.

You know my predicament, Lord. On the one hand, the person of Jesus Christ has had a huge impact on my spiritual journey. You know that I have been in tears of joy declaring Jesus as my Lord and Saviour from a place of complete brokenness and humility. You know the hours I have spent on my knees, writing out passages of Scripture and begging You for mercy. You know that through obedience I have repented and been baptised both in water and in the Holy Spirit. You also know that I have struggled intensely with the contradictions concerning Your sovereignty and 'free will' that affect so many central Christian doctrines.

Although I have withdrawn somewhat from the Christian faith, I don't believe I have done so due to pride, because I am still petrified of Your power and the fact that You could make me suffer endlessly and excruciatingly if that were Your will. My problems with the Christian faith come from a place of earnestly seeking after Truth.

I would much rather sell all my possessions and lead an itinerant life sharing the gospel than end up in hell. Truly! There are no benefits to living outside of the Christian faith, other than a few carnal pleasures that one can enjoy when one is not concerned about sin. But You know, Lord, that I have fasted and continue to fast, and that I strive to live a holy life and flee from sin, and that the pleasures of this world are hardly tempting to me in comparison to paradise after death.

Logically, I should be a Christian. But I don't know that I can do it. I have been a Christian, and totally immersed in Christian evangelism, serving in church, attending house groups, studying the Bible, being sacrificial, believing in Jesus, praying and worshiping, and loving the peace and joy that come with being His disciple. But every time I have thrown myself wholeheartedly into the Christian life, the contradictions and inconsistencies of Christian thinking have risen to the surface of my mind and taken hold of me with great force, causing me to draw back from the faith.

Surely, Lord, these doubts come from You. Christians will deny that, and this is one of the reasons why I can't be a Christian, because Christians pick and choose which thoughts and beliefs come from You and which come from our own 'free will' or the devil. I *know* that You are in control of all things, Lord, and I'm grateful that You have given me that understanding. But it is not the Christian understanding!

I know that life is so much more meaningful when living for Jesus. I cannot see any meaning outside of the Christian life. And yet it seems, for whatever reason, that You won't allow me to fully submit my life in that way. You have made certain aspects of reality plain to me; things that most Christians fail to see, and this is both a blessing and a curse.

The plain truth is that we do not have free will! If any Christian is reading this and wants to tell me that my destiny is up to me and not You... well, You know the truth, Lord. You know that Christians pray to You about their lives; their jobs, their health, their marriages; knowing full well that You are in control of every aspect of their lives. Prayer would make no sense if this were not true.

I beg of You, Lord, don't send me to hell. It would only demonstrate cruelty. Again, Christians will disagree with this and say You would be perfectly just sending me to hell because I am a sinner. But You know the truth, Lord, that I have never done anything that has not been completely under

Your control. It's so obvious to me that this is true. How would I know how to manufacture thoughts, beat my heart, circulate my blood, digest my food, dream, grow my hair, grow from a baby into an adult, or do anything else? It is absurd to think that I am in control of myself! And yet Christians cannot see this, and refuse to consider any position that compromises freedom of the human will.

Perhaps I should suppress the truth and become a Christian? Okay, Lord, I will. If that's what You want. If it will save me from hell. But You are in control, so You have to make it happen. Or do You have other plans for me? Can I not be a Christian and still escape hell somehow? Because You are sovereign, I believe it's within Your power to do whatever You want with my mind, body, and soul. So would You please, please, be merciful to me, Lord, and not make me suffer torment in hell? Please, Lord?

> *I form the light and create darkness, I bring prosperity and create disaster; I, the LORD, do all these things.* (Isaiah 45:7)

> *I know, O LORD, that the way of man is not in himself, that it is not in man who walks to direct his steps.* (Jeremiah 10:23)

✣ 97 ✣

HOW WE GOT THE BIBLE

19th April 2018

In my efforts to better understand how the text of the Bible came to be as it is today, I'm currently reading a book entitled 'How We Got the Bible' by Neil R. Lightfoot. A passage I was reading today stood out, and I would like to share it, as I think it highlights a flaw in the thought of many Christians concerning God's relationship with human beings.

In the ninth chapter of the book (p 95), Lightfoot writes the following:

> *It is a fact that the New Testament text has been transmitted to us through the hands of copyists. It is also a fact that, since these hands were human, they were susceptible to the slips and faults of all human hands.* **It is not true, therefore, that God has guided the many different scribes in their tasks of copying the Sacred Scriptures.** *The Scrip-*

316

tures, although divine, have been handed down through the centuries by means of copies, just like any other ancient book. (emphasis added)

I find this reasoning to be problematic. If God was not involved in the process of scribes copying manuscripts, it is illogical to say that it is by God's providence that we have the Bible in the form(s) it takes today. To take God out of the lives of the scribes is to remove God from the history of human activity and deny His ability to unfold the events of history in the way He chooses.

It would make much more sense to say that God is in sovereign control of His creation, and that He was in control of the copying process embarked upon by the scribes. That way, we can say with full confidence that when we are reading the Bible the words on the page are as God intended them to be. The fact that there are errors and contested readings is a part of God's plan, as He doesn't like humans to be perfect in every way all the time.

Theologians have a clear choice to consider. Either God is sovereign over creation and we can read the Bible knowing that we are reading the words God intended for us to read, or if we maintain that God was not guiding the scribes, as Lightfoot suggests, our confidence in reading evaporates and chance and circumstance necessarily come into the equation, depriving God of His sovereignty and depriving our modern Bibles of their authority.

98

UNCONDITIONAL LOVE

7th June 2018

In this post I'd like to share a few thoughts about love, and specifically how love operates in the life of a Christian. I will argue that the Christian worldview presents a God who loves conditionally, and that this fails to satisfy our innate longing for unconditional love.

We have in the New Testament a wonderful definition of love given by the apostle Paul in 1 Corinthians 13. He says the following:

> *4 Love is patient, love is kind. It does not envy, it does not boast, it is not proud. 5 It does not dishonour others, it is not self-seeking, it is not easily angered, it keeps no record of wrongs. 6 Love does not delight in evil but rejoices with the truth. 7 It always protects, always trusts, always hopes, always perseveres.*

It's interesting that Paul says love keeps no record of wrongs, as within the Christian worldview we all deserve punishment from God for our wrongs. It would seem that Paul's definition of love doesn't apply to God. In response to this point the Christian might say Jesus' function is to erase the wrongs of *those who turn from their sin and follow Him*.

That's the condition that we need to meet to be deserving of God's love.

In the above scripture, Paul also says that love does not delight in evil, which makes me wonder whether God is delighting in evil when He casts unbelievers into the lake of fire (Revelation 20:15). Of course, many Christians present the argument that God's justice somehow *demands* that He must send unbelievers to hell, but this is a ridiculous argument because God is in control of all things and can do whatever He pleases. He is not compelled to do anything – that's what makes Him God.

According to the Christian worldview, the only way to avoid God's wrath and punishment is to obey the commands of Christ (see John 14:21).

God's love is not unconditional, but conditional.

This puts the Christian in a rather difficult position, because during evangelistic activities he/she is compelled to convey the *conditional* love of God (with a warning about damnation), rather than unconditional love. I believe this creates an awkward tension, and is necessarily divisive. I believe people are often dismissive of Christians because the message of love is conditional, while we all have an innate desire to experience unconditional love. I believe this is the reason why a lot of the time people resist the call the follow Jesus.

Of course, Jesus knew that His message would be divisive (see Luke 12:51-52).

I don't think there's any escaping the fact that the Christian worldview presents a God who is hostile towards some people. An alternative worldview would be one where every being is loved unconditionally by God, and in which Buddhists, Hindus, Sikhs, Bahá'ís, and others, all have an important role to play in God's grand plan, which He is unfolding in accordance with His sovereign will. From this perspective, every human being has a purpose and a unique calling, not only those who choose to follow Christ. While each individual journey may involve suffering as part of God's intricately crafted plan, He eventually liberates everyone.

That would be unconditional love.

✺ 99 ✺

EVERYDAY MYSTERIES

14th June 2018

True philosophy is about a fascination with all that is mysterious in life. That's why I have studied, and continue to study, philosophy; because I find it ceaselessly intriguing thinking about why we are here, what reality is, why we suffer, the nature of God, and other such questions that tap into the heart of the mystery.

One philosopher who I feel a real affinity with (because he thinks in a similar way about philosophy) is Brian Magee. Magee is a British philosopher who was educated at Oxford and mingled with some of the leading philosophers of the 20th Century, including Karl Popper, Bertrand Russell, and many others.

I'm currently reading Magee's autobiography, and reading the first few pages I felt I could personally relate to his fascination with the simple everyday things most people take for granted. I will quote a passage from the book to give you an example:

> I retain a vivid memory of myself... when I was seven or eight, standing in a shaft of sunlight in the corner of the kitchen by our back door... focusing my eyes keenly on the index finger of my right hand, which I held pointed upwards in front of my face. *I'm going to count to three*, I was saying to myself, *and when I say 'three' my finger's going to bend.* Then I counted: *One, two, thr—* And sure enough on *three* my finger bent. How did I do it? I did it again. Then I thought: *This time I'll count to four.* And on *four* my finger bent. Next time I counted to five. My finger bent on *five*. I tried dragging out the counting so as to catch my finger out: *one, two... three... four... {wait for it}... five!* But on *five* my finger, not caught napping at all, bent. I could bend my finger whenever I liked. Or not, just as I decided. Yet no matter how hard I concentrated I couldn't grasp anything at all about how I did it. How could something that was so completely within my command, solely and entirely a matter of my own conscious decision, be a nothing for me, just simply no experience whatever, and yet happen? From that day to this the problem has fascinated me.
>
> (Magee, B., *Confessions of a Philosopher*, Random House, 1997, p 1-2).

In a way similar to Magee's fascination with his ability to make his finger bend, during the height of my spiritual explorations I became fascinated with thought. I was spending a lot of time in meditation, a process which encouraged me to watch thoughts arising in my mind. I remember one day being sat on my bed and deciding to really closely investigate what a thought is and where my thoughts were coming from.

It was investigations such as this that led me to an awareness that there is a power making my thoughts arise, and that was a real revelation to me. It couldn't be *me* making my thoughts arise because I couldn't predict them, nor could I understand how I was making them arise. By thinking the problem through I arrived at the understanding that God must be bringing my thoughts into existence, and in the same way as God is making my thoughts arise, I realised He must also be in control of all the other processes I experience as part of my aliveness.

I believe that understanding the omnipresence of God provides the solution to the problem that fascinated Magee, who, being an atheist, would never have accepted that God was the answer to the finger-bending mystery.

100

IS PHILOSOPHY IMPORTANT?

5th July 2018

It's interesting how within spiritual circles there are strong and conflicting opinions about the importance of philosophy. I know that many Christians feel the subject is a waste of time, and instead focus exclusively on Biblical revelation as life's only real source of wisdom. On the other hand, there are many who feel philosophy and religion go hand in hand, and that it is impossible to defend one's faith without engaging in philosophy at least on some level.

In this article I will briefly explain why philosophy is important to me, and why as much as I have immersed myself in Christian living, I have never been able to dismiss the importance of philosophical enquiry.

What is Philosophy?

I think that often philosophy can seem like a subject that is highly academic; full of propositions and logic and complex arguments that would give anyone a headache. But for me, this is not what philosophy is at all.

Philosophy is the quest to understand the true nature of reality, including ourselves.

Philosophy, for me, begins with fascination and mystery. It starts with the astonishing fact that I find myself in some kind of *existence* doing something called *living*, and I seem to experience things like the functioning of my body, mind, and emotions, as well as being aware of a universe that I can observe.

Ever since lying in the bath for hours during my time at university listening to talks by the comparative religion philosopher Alan Watts, I have been excited to try to understand why I am here, what exactly I am, and why anything exists at all.

Can We Really Know Anything?

I have found that through the exploration of many different spiritual paths and philosophical viewpoints, I have been able to answer a lot of the questions that first troubled me when I began to deeply ponder the nature of reality during my time at university.

It has been a long and difficult journey, but through reading the ideas of deep-thinking people, and more importantly examining the answers to philosophical questions for myself, I have been able to form a worldview that makes sense to me, feels honest and truthful, and gives meaning to my life.

How Did I Get There?

Without a doubt my biggest discovery was that God exists. As a youngster I was an ardent atheist, and the idea of God seemed very illogical and even frustrating. I used to be angered by the seemingly ridiculous faith some people had in an entity that for me was no more real than unicorns.

The thing about God is that He reveals Himself to people in His own time and in His own way.

For me, the revelation of God's existence came during a spell in psychiatric hospital. I had been desperately searching for meaning and truth for years, immersing myself in the spiritual practices of different faith groups, but only experiencing confusion, hopelessness, longing, and desperation.

When I eventually ended up in hospital after a serious breakdown, I felt compelled to ask the staff for a Bible, which would have been a complete surprise to those who knew me, as I had never taken a serious interest in Christianity before. But God used the Bible and my time in hospital to awaken me to His presence. He began to speak to me and show me that He is in control of my life.

Christianity, for me, was a huge awakening. But it didn't answer all of the questions that I had about the nature of God and reality. I discovered that Christians were unable to answer fundamental questions about the relationship between God and human beings. There were contradictions and confusions in the Christian worldview that I simply couldn't ignore.

I ended up writing several books that expound what I have come to understand about God, and these books deal with those questions to which I have found Christians have no satisfying answers.

Conclusion

It is not my intention to in any way belittle the Christian faith. I have been a dedicated evangelical Christian in the past and made the Bible the focus of my life for many years, so I completely understand the passion with which Christians dedicate themselves to their faith. I also fully understand the fear Christians have of being drawn away from Jesus – that's a fear I have felt myself on many occasions.

But for me, there are philosophical problems with the Christian worldview that are very significant. For instance, I have come to understand that God is in control of everything that happens, which is something a Christian cannot agree with as the whole Christian worldview hinges on freedom of the human will. This is a very significant problem and the implications are manifold.

It is through a joint exploration of faith and philosophy that I have been able to answer my deepest questions. Reading the Bible encouraged me to believe in God, but philosophical enquiry proved to me that without doubt there is a God, and taught me deep truths about who and what God is, and how those truths relate to my own existence and the existence of the world I experience. So that's why I am happy to argue that philosophy is important.

101

IS MEDITATION GOOD FOR YOU?

14th September 2018

Meditation has been a huge part of my spiritual journey. I have been on various meditation retreats and spent long periods practising mindfulness (even before it was fashionable!) and focusing on what is often referred to as 'living in the now'. But is any of this really helpful? Here are a few reflections.

Being Grounded is Important

It's possible to be so carried away in thought that we become out of touch with our bodies and immediate surroundings. Being in tune with our bodies helps us to stay healthy, and being in tune with our immediate surroundings helps us to be more relaxed, and at peace. If you experience a lot of stress, live a life that is very fast-paced, or have mental health issues, meditation could certainly be beneficial.

Don't Meditate to Become 'Enlightened'

If you're attracted to meditation because you want to experience 'Christ consciousness' or some other deep state of spiritual awakening, you're going to be disappointed. Often people begin meditation practice as a form of escape, and the alluring idea of enlightenment has a strong pull for spiritually-inclined people. But as I explained in depth in my book *The Philosophy of a Mad Man*, there is no enlightenment. You may experience more peace and a greater awareness, but if you're looking for a grand mystical experience that will free you from your troubles, you're taking the wrong approach. Psychotherapy or counselling are likely to be a much better option.

How do I get Started with Meditation?

There are of course many different ways in which to meditate, and I would encourage you to explore different approaches and methods and see what appeals. By far my favourite meditation technique is Autogenic Training, which has helped me to counteract the onset of panic attacks, as well as to destress in times of personal difficulty.

One way of getting started with meditation without having to learn anything is to try simply sitting or lying in a quiet space and focusing on the sensation of your feet. Whenever your thoughts wander, return your awareness to the feeling you are experiencing in your feet. Do this for 10-15 minutes and you might be surprised by how relaxed you feel.

Is Meditation Compatible with Religion?

Of course, in certain Eastern religions, meditation is central. For Christians, things are rather more complicated. Prayer is itself a form of meditation, and many Christians will feel that prayer is the most important and most effective way in which to impact our circumstances. In my own experience, the practice of focusing deeply on my thoughts gave me a greater awareness of the existence of God, and while this isn't necessarily typical, meditation is complementary to philosophy and religion in that we are exploring the nature of our experiences and what it means to be alive.

Conclusion

The word 'meditation' encompasses a variety of practices that are focused on making us more aware and in tune with how our minds and bodies function. If you're just starting out, be aware of your motivations for wanting to meditate, and consider whether talking therapy might be more beneficial, or at least complementary to your meditation practice. Don't expect miracles, but a small regular time commitment to a meditative practice can reap great rewards and contribute to a more balanced, happy life.

❧ 102 ❧

THE BLESSING DILEMMA

9th October 2018

Is it truly more blessed to give than to receive? In this post I'd like to offer a few thoughts on this dilemma by recalling a situation I'm sure many of you will have encountered in daily life.

Love is a word at the heart of the Christian faith, as exemplified by the two commandments that Jesus said are the most important:

> [36] *"Teacher, which is the greatest commandment in the Law?"*
> [37] *Jesus replied: "'Love the Lord your God with all your heart and with all your soul and with all your mind.' [38] This is the first and greatest commandment. [39] And the second is like it: 'Love your neighbour as yourself.' [40] All the Law and the Prophets hang on these two commandments."*
> (Matthew 22:36-40 NIV)

So we are to love God and love our neighbour. But how does one's obedience to the second of these commandments, to love our neighbour, play out in the theatre of life?

One scripture that provides some guidance is Acts 20:35, in which Paul quotes Jesus as saying "It is more blessed to give than to receive". The context of the passage is that Paul is speaking to the leaders of the church in Ephesus (while on his missionary travels), giving examples of how to live with humility and serve the Lord.

But how does Jesus' statement, recalled by Paul, apply to us today?

Let's look at a practical example. Say you've gone out for a meal with a friend, and when it's time to pay the bill a conversation must be had concerning who's going to pay. You offer to pay, believing that the gesture would demonstrate kindness. Your friend responds by offering to pay, as they wish to be kind to you. At this point the blessing dilemma arises:

Is it more of a blessing to the other person for you to pay, or to let them pay?

It seems to me that the only way to 'win' in this situation is to reach a compromise. For example, one person can pay but with the agreement that the other will pay the next time you meet up. Or some other compromise can be struck; perhaps you split the bill or the one who doesn't pay for the meal agrees to pay for the taxi home.

I suppose the main point I'd like to make in this article is that while we may feel generosity is instinctively an act of giving, we always have to be aware that if we are too generous, we may actually be hurting the feelings of others by making them feel guilty. Wherever possible, compromise seems to be the best way to be as loving as possible.

GEOFFREY PARRINDER:
INTERFAITH MASTER

13th November 2018

I've been interested in comparative religion ever since my university days, when I used to spend hours listening to recordings of talks given by the philosopher Alan Watts. Watts, with his knack for communicating Zen paradoxes, has these days become somewhat of a cult figure in spiritual circles.

After joining a central London library a few weeks ago I felt eager to explore the Religion section, and was delighted to find a couple of shelves dedicated entirely to works of comparative religion. I'm sure the contents of these books could keep me entertained for years, but in this post I just want to talk briefly about one book which has been a delight to read, and which I would highly recommend.

The book is entitled *Upanishads, Gita, and Bible* and was written in 1962 by an English philosopher named Geoffrey Parrinder. I was unable to find out much about the author, except that he was a Methodist minister for some time, published around 30 books in his lifetime, and was active as a professor at Kings College London until 1977. He also undertook extensive missionary work in West Africa.

When reading his book, I had no idea whether Parrinder was writing from a Christian, Hindu, or other standpoint, such was the impressive impartiality of his writing. It was only after finishing the book that I discovered he had been a Christian minister.

The book's structure is clear and intuitive. It begins with a comparison of the creation stories of the Bible and the Indian religions, before proceeding to tackle many of the key topics of fruitful interfaith dialogue, including 'The One and the Many', 'What is Man?', 'Immortality', 'Mysticism', 'Conduct and Suffering', and a few others. The subject matter is tackled with a great depth of knowledge, and as I read the book I felt as though each paragraph had been carefully and thoughtfully constructed, with no words wasted.

There were a few insights in the book that really struck me, and which I believe will stay with me for years to come. By way of example, I will share three insights that really stood out for me.

1. Parrinder points out that the Bible, and in particular the Old Testament, is very sketchy when it comes to the idea of souls. This is something that has occurred to me in the past, and I once wrote an essay on the subject. It is very difficult to

discern what a soul might be from what is written in the Torah.

2. The author used a phrase that really struck me. He described the human experience as being a journey 'from the alone to the Alone'. This captures something very beautiful about Eastern spirituality; the idea that the individual, upon death, is absorbed into the being of God. This short phrase expresses the relationship between the Atman (the human soul) and Brahman (the universal soul).

3. Another beautiful concept from the book is that the Eastern religions have an 'I-it' relationship with God, whereas the Abrahamic religions have an 'I-Thou' relationship with the divine. The difference, of course, is that in the first example God is not personal, whereas He is in the second. This is an important distinction between Hinduism and the Abrahamic religions, and a fascinating point for interfaith discussion.

I know that among the readers of this blog there are many Christians who are very sceptical of non-Christian religious traditions. I do understand and respect that, having been an evangelical Christian myself in the past. But I would suggest that to open one's mind to the beliefs of billions of people who have lived and died outside of the Christian faith is a wonderfully enriching thing to do.

VIII

2019

❧ 104 ❧

DEBUNKING THE LAW OF ATTRACTION

9th June 2019

If you're interested in spirituality to any extent, it's likely that you've come across people speaking about the 'law of attraction'. In this post, I'll be offering some thoughts about this phenomenon and explaining why I believe the idea makes mistaken assumptions about the nature of reality.

What is the Law of Attraction?

Back in 2006, a book entitled *The Secret* was released. The book was an accompaniment to a film of the same name, and brought the idea of the law of attraction to a mainstream audience. To give you some idea of the impact of the book and film, the book has been translated into thirty different languages and sold over 50 million copies.

The idea promulgated by the book and film can be concisely expressed as follows:

As your thought radiates out, it attracts the energy and
frequencies of like thoughts, like objects, and even like people,
and draws those things back to you.
(https://www.thesecret.tv/law-of-attraction/)

It's easy to see why the idea has had such a huge impact. It is a tremendously empowering concept, making the individual feel they have control over what happens in their lives, and by extension providing the liberating feeling that it's possible to have whatever you want in life, if you can only control your thoughts in the correct manner.

Why is the Law of Attraction such a popular idea?

The idea has cemented itself deeply in the New Age spiritual movement, and you only need to do a search on social media to see this for yourself. To offer one example, I recently saw someone on Instagram claiming that they manifested themself a new bike within a week, purely via the power of positive thinking.

When people don't believe in God, there is necessarily a great deal of mystery to existence. This feeling of mystery leaves people vulnerable to embracing any idea that seems to make sense of reality, however strange and outlandish the idea might be. This is the reason why cults are able to prosper — and many do within the New Age spiritual movement — because uncertainty about our place in the grand scheme of things leaves people vulnerable to ideological manipulation.

I believe the reason why *The Secret* has been so successful is that it taps into that deep sense of mystery, providing an explanation for how reality works that can be enticing and reassuring.

So What's Wrong with the Law of Attraction?

In a word, the problem with the idea is that it is *Godless*. Spiritual seekers get very excited when they experience synchronicity in their lives, as this would seem to be evidence that they have some mastery over the law of attraction. However, despite regularly asking 'the universe' for things, 'the universe' is not considered by these people to be a personal being in the way God is understood to be in the Abrahamic religions, for instance.

The problem with seeing the universe as an object in this way is that it doesn't really explain anything. To really understand why synchronistic events happen in our lives, we need to understand that an omnipresent and personal God exists, and that this God is unfolding all events in creation. When we understand this, it solves the problem which *The Secret* begins to tap into but doesn't really solve in a deep and satisfying way.

Why Believe in God?

Of course, if someone has had no revelation of the reality of God, they may feel they have no good grounds to believe such a being exists. God doesn't reveal Himself to everyone all of the time, but instead employs a kind of veil over the minds of many, which prevents them from being aware of Him. But when He does reveal Himself, He does so in very tangible ways, like speaking directly to the minds of human beings and working miracles.

Conclusion

To really understand why events in the universe unfold in the way they do, we need to focus on God. Even if someone is convinced that the law of attraction works, the bigger question of *why it works* remains. The answer to the problem of *why* any events occur within the created universe is that a living and personal God exists, and He is actively controlling everything that happens in the eternal present moment.

If you're reading this and the idea of God's existence seems unlikely to you, why not pray for Him to reveal Himself to you? What have you got to lose? If there is no God, then you've wasted only a prayer, but if there is a God (and God chooses to reveal Himself to you), then you will have at last found a solution to life's biggest mysteries in a way that is much more satisfying than the vague and misguided solution offered by books such as *The Secret*.

Of course, once you know God exists, there is the further question of what kind of god He is — the Christian God, the Muslim God, a Hindu god, or some other god? I invite you to read my book entitled *God's Grand Game: Divine Sovereignty and the Cosmic Playground*, which was written with the intention of helping spiritual seekers grapple with all of life's big questions.

105

LIFE: TRAGEDY OR COMEDY?

11th September 2019

The book of Ecclesiastes in the Bible talks about how every-thing that happens has already happened before, and that there is nothing new under the sun. If this is true, it might be immensely frustrating for God. For if God cannot do anything new, how can He remain inspired, excited, and stimulated for billions upon billions of years?

I find in creation significant evidence that God has been playing the game of life for an extremely long time. When we look, for instance, at the way global affairs unfold, and the way technology advances, there is a gradual and systematic unfolding of the events in history that is surely the work of an experienced Master Craftsman.

Consider for a moment the history of the last two thousand years, and the billions of people who have lived and died in that time, all contributing something different to God's plan for Earth. And then consider that we are inhabitants of one planet out of possibly billions. The story of the universe is so epic that it puts a Tolkien or Lucas story to shame.

The countless stories within stories, and the way in which complex and diverse storylines fit together in the microcosm and the macrocosm, reveal a kind of intelligence so vast that it baffles the mind. And yet, I suspect that the story of the entire evolution of our planet is a relatively simple thing to God, because where we experience novelty and change, really God is employing the same techniques over and over again with only superficial variations. This might be compared to an aged composer who, having studied the intervals between notes for a lifetime, has become a master of the mechanics of the way in which musical notes communicate, and is able to churn out song after song with great ease.

If God has essentially created everything which it is possible to create, I consider that there are two possibilities. One is that God is bored to the point of agony, and yet continues to create simply for something to do. This would be rather tragic. The other possibility is that creation forever remains an interesting, exciting, and joyful process for God, and that He delights ceaselessly in the new iterations of beings and things that He creates. This would make life more of a comedy.

Which of these two possibilities represents the truth about God is possibly the single most important question for philosophically inclined theologians to consider. For if God suffers, it makes sense that we suffer, because God has frustration which He needs to vent. On the other hand, if God doesn't suffer, and all is perpetually joyful for Him, then our suffering is much more likely to be only a stepping stone towards a happy resolution which God will manifest — and that we will enjoy — at a time in the future when our particular storyline in God's Grand Game is brought to a conclusion.

106

YOUR PAST DOES NOT DETERMINE YOUR FUTURE

15th September 2019

A popular idea within the scientific community is that what happens in the present moment is the result of a chain of causes and effects. This deeply ingrained idea is what prompted scientists to come up with the 'Big Bang' theory — the idea that a single event, at the beginning of time, is the cause of everything we experience today.

There is an obvious problem with this theory. If time is a linear process, then it seems natural to ask what existed before the moment when the universe, for whatever reason, exploded into being. Much ink has been spilled by scientists trying to find an argument that makes sense of the idea that this vast and complex universe could spontaneously emerge out of absolute nothingness (or some kind of quantum vacuum).

An alternative view of reality — and this is the view that I subscribe to — is that the entirety of existence is contained within God. God has the attribute of aseity, which means He is self-existing, so there has never been a time when God didn't exist. Actually, all that exists right now, in this moment, is not the result of cause and effect; instead, what we experience as present-moment reality is the manifestation of a living God.

If a living God is the animator of all events in existence, then it is not the case that events unfold in some kind of mechanical process of cause and effect. Instead, existence is much more fluid and rather like a puppet show, in which God is unfolding a story which could go in any direction that He wills in any given moment. If this perspective is correct, it means that the past does not define the future, and that in any given moment there are infinite possibilities open to God, and He always has the option of unfolding events in whichever way He chooses.

So, the two thoughts I'd like to leave you with today are as follows:

1. The past does not determine the future
2. God is in control of existence in its entirety

If you understand my thinking on this subject, these two statements should be very liberating for you. They are empowering ideas, in a sense, because they imply that the future is unwritten, and that your prayers and actions therefore have the potential to literally change the course of history.

Of course, what you pray about, and what you do, will happen only if they are a part of God's will. I'm well aware that this raises the question of whether or not humans have free will, and I have dedicated most of my adult life to exploring the philosophical implications that result from my perspective that there is a single living God who is in control of all activity in existence — a perspective explored in my book *God's Grand Game*.

107

YOU NEVER KNOW (POEM)

28th October 2019

You never know when someone

May catch a dream from you

You never know when a little word

Or something you might do

May open up a window

Of the mind that seeks the light

The way you live might not matter at all

But then again it might.

It might.

· · ·

And just in case it could be

That another's life through you

Could possibly change for better

With a broader brighter view

It seems it might be worth a try

At pointing the way to right

Of course it might not matter at all

But then again it might.

It might.

And one day when I'm older

And my life is nearly through

I'll reminisce over challenges

And the light that got me through

I'll know I've always done by best

To follow the road that's right

The way I lived might not matter at all

But then again it might.

It might.

❧ 108 ❧

NOUGHTS AND ONES

31st October 2019

It's no secret that I have significant fears about the role of technology in our lives. Those of you who have listened to my song *Machines Taking Over the World* will know this is a big issue for me.

Well, today I had someone come to my flat to fix a problem in the bathroom. Before he carried out the work (it was a very simple fix) he got a tablet out of his bag and started answering questions on the screen. He voiced his frustration at the fact that, even as a plumber, the digital world has made his job more difficult in certain ways.

I voiced my sympathy with the plumber, and said the following:

The problem with technology, and machines, is that they make every-thing black and white, whereas in reality, life isn't black and white.

I think this argument sums up why machines will never be able to do so many things as well as human beings. Scientists often get very enthusiastic about the capabilities of artificial intelligence to carry out a range of tasks, but anyone who has ever used technology will appreciate that it goes wrong so much of the time for this exact reason: organic beings do not do things in binary ways. There are always infinite possibilities regarding how events can unfold in any given situation. Computers simply can't cope with that, and they never will be able to.

Now I'm not anti-technology *per se*; I love my MacBook and my iPhone which improve my life in many ways. But I will keep making the argument that technology should be employed in a strictly limited and controlled way if we are to avoid colossal societal catastrophes in the future due to a simple 'nought' or 'one' being out of place somewhere.

The over-excitement that many tech enthusiasts feel about artificial intelligence makes me very angry, because I can clearly see that these people haven't fully considered the consequences of their actions. Making machines that are ever more powerful is something that many people lust over, but it's a kind of insanity that may prove catastrophic in the near future if we're not careful. We have to learn to use technology only when it is advantageous to human (or creaturely) flourishing, not just because it boosts our egos to know that we have created something powerful.

109

WHY ARE YOU CRUEL, LORD?

4th November 2019

I feel incredibly frustrated and rather angry. All I want is to feel peace and joy. I know, Lord God, that You could grant this for me easily. I have suffered too much, Lord, and I don't want to harm or enslave or punish anyone, all I want is peace.

I'm so tired of struggling, Lord, of all the depression and fear and confusion. I don't know what the solution is, except I know how very easy it would be for You to grant me this and answer my prayers.

You are in control of all things, Lord, and You choose to make me suffer. It's so frustrating, Lord. Why are You cruel, Lord? I honestly don't understand. It seems so unnecessary. Have You created us only to make us suffer, Lord? Why would You be so cruel?

Please, God, reconsider. Choose peace and love and mercy, over fear, anxiety, frustration, and punishment. I know I must trust in Your wisdom, Lord. But I've had enough. I want my suffering to end.

110

THE MADNESS OF SCIENCE

7th November 2019

Scientific exploration, particularly in the domain of physics, can be summarised as the investigation into *what causes what*. Hugely influential ideas in the contemporary scientific paradigm, such as evolution, genetics, and the Big Bang theory, all have this methodology at their core.

According to my own philosophical perspective, however, there is one cause of all supposedly differentiated processes, which is God. From this viewpoint, the past doesn't cause the future, but instead there is only a present moment unfolding in which change, wherever it takes place, is directed and animated by God.

This perspective, a kind of 'occasionalism', says that an event will only happen on any occasion if God wills and directs it to take place. The so-called 'laws of physics' are not absolute, and can be overruled by God at any time, which is what happens in the case of events that religious people often describe as miracles.

The *cause and effect* paradigm has become deeply embedded in the contemporary zeitgeist, so that we speak about nearly every event in terms of what caused it. But this is a kind of madness — if I choose to do a little dance around my living room right now, could anyone seriously argue that my every gesture is merely the result of a chain of causes and effects leading back to the first moment of our universe's creation?

Surely, such a perspective is wildly irrational. The correct perspective is radically different: *The solution to the scientific problem of what causes what is simply that God causes everything.* I wholeheartedly believe this to be true, and if you closely examine and meditate upon your present moment experience, you may discover this truth for yourself.

III

HUMANE PRISONS

20th November 2019

While searching an online video platform today, I stumbled upon something which had a profound impact on me. I have for many years been a supporter of the idea of a justice system that rehabilitates rather than punishes. As I explained in my 2012 article entitled *Compassionate Justice*, I feel that aggressive forms of punishment for criminals only continue the cycle of bullying, fear, anger, and hatred, and do little to rectify society's ills.

When I spotted a video this evening entitled *How Norway Designed a More Humane Prison*, my interest was piqued. I think that the idea of compassionate justice is so alien to us in the West that I had never really considered places of imprisonment could be humane to this degree.

What the video made me realise is that so much of what I struggle with on a daily basis comes from fear of the kind of violence and oppression that is commonplace in prisons in Britain and America. Please don't get me wrong. I haven't committed any crimes. But I realised I have been living for many years with a subconscious fear of accidentally breaking the law in some way and ending up in a prison where I would suffer violence and intimidation.

If Britain were to introduce prisons of the kind featured in the video I watched, where inmates are treated with respect and compassion, it would be liberating in a way that could be really transformative. That underlying sense of fear – which is perpetuated by the media and politicians – would be lifted, and I for one would feel so much freer; *not free to commit crimes*, but free to simply relax and focus on contributing to society in a positive way. I feel that without the fear of harsh imprisonment most of us would be kinder and better people, because, paradoxically, fear of being bullied is actually the cause of most bullying.

After watching the video about the humane prison in Norway, I immediately feel more motivated to campaign for humane prisons in the UK, and I really hope some of my American readers will do the same, because I know rates of incarceration in the United States are especially high.

As I write this article, I have a vision of a future where populations do not live in fear of punishment, and where this actually *reduces rather than increases* crime. This is huge shift in perspective for me. I'm realising that prisons are a major cause of crime rather than functioning to prevent it. I thank God for the revelation.

MENTAL ILLNESS AND THE CHEMICAL IMBALANCE MYTH

30th November 2019

I believe that what are currently diagnosed as mental illnesses should be seen as expressions of character or personality rather than brain disorders. The way in which we behave could only be described as a brain disorder if the reality is that chemicals in our brains control our personalities. But I'm quite sure this isn't the case. Please allow me to explain how I have arrived at this conclusion.

If the way we behave is merely the result of chemicals operating in our brains, one would have to ask the question of what is causing this chemical activity. One argument might be that our brains are like machines, but if this is the case we would have to ask, who built the machines and what is controlling their activity?

The philosophy of materialism has led many to believe that our brains are autonomous. From this perspective, we are no different to robots who have been programmed in a certain way. Those who believe in such a vision argue that our behaviour is due to our genetic makeup and evolution, but nothing more. This reality construct leads scientists to see everything that happens as a cause and effect process which began in a single moment, when the universe came into being due to a 'Big Bang' event. This view attempts to exclude God entirely.

I believe the truth of the matter is that all human beings are created and animated by a living God. So there is a spiritual component to our personalities which, despite being a reality, is not even considered by most doctors and scientists who promote a materialistic view of reality.

It's easy to see how the materialist ideology came about if one considers that the proponents of these theories have not had a revelation of the reality of God, and also have the incentive that they can make a lot of money from promoting the 'brain as machine' myth. Pharmaceutical companies have become very rich by exploiting the ignorance of patients who will simply believe the 'chemical imbalance' myth, trusting in their doctor's supposed wisdom and not questioning whether the philosophical arguments made by doctors and neuroscientists are sound.

I'm quite convinced that the scientific paradigm which has led to the chemical imbalance theory of mental illness is very misguided. In reality, all of the activity that we experience in our bodies and minds is brought about by God, who is animating all activity in existence. God is omnipresent and in control of everything that happens. Causes and effects only happen on a particular occasion if God actively brings them about.

Sometimes people experience extremes of behaviour which can be dangerous, and there may be a role for medication in dealing with these. However, the medication I'm referring to should not be prescribed with the aim of correcting chemical imbalances, but instead it should aim at helping to restore a healthy equilibrium in the personalities of those whose behaviour might be considered dangerous. For instance, if someone is experiencing a very elated mood, they might be prescribed a medication like Diazepam which could have the effect of relaxing them. If someone is deeply depressed, a small amount of MDMA could be prescribed in order to lift their mood.

Currently, psychiatric medication has horrendous side effects, and the medication doesn't work effectively in most cases. Mental health patients often become like zombies and suffer terribly. Once again, this is because the medications are designed to alter 'chemical imbalances', when really chemicals are not the cause of our behaviour — God is.

Those reading this article might not understand why I believe that God is the cause of all human activity. A complete over-view of this perspective can be found in my 2019 book release entitled *God's Grand Game: Divine Sovereignty and the Cosmic Playground.*

I believe that healthcare should primarily be about compassion and love. I believe that when the free-for-everyone

National Health Service was established in the United Kingdom in 1948, this was the vision of its founders in the Labour Party. They wanted to help reduce suffering rather than profit from it.

There is, of course, an important role for doctors, nurses, and other health workers in helping to reduce suffering. But the world of healthcare has become so corrupt that this noble aim has been almost entirely neglected, and because elements of our healthcare system are run for profit rather than genuine compassion, patients are abused and suffer terribly.

Of course, when it comes to the way reality has unfolded, and continues to unfold, nothing has happened or can happen aside from the will of God. Where there have been abuses in the system, these have not taken place outside of the will of God, who is sovereign over all events. The fact is, God includes suffering in His plans for creation. I have described some reasons as to why this might be the case in *God's Grand Game*.

My prayer is that God will bring enlightenment to those who work in healthcare around the world, and that the suffering of people who have been boxed-in and abused by the mental health system will end. If you agree with me, please say a prayer and ask God to bring about reforms for the better.

❧ 113 ❧

THE FUTURE IS TERRIFYING

8th December 2019

It's currently 3am and I haven't gone to bed yet. I've been watching videos online about technological innovation. It's absolutely staggering what machines are doing these days, and the scope of their applications is frightening – there are even startup companies trying to engineer biology in various ways.

It seems that in the last couple of years there has been an explosion in these areas. It feels as though God has been completely forgotten about. Arrogant scientists disregard God as though He is a ridiculous fiction. One of the reasons I want to start a new forward thinking church is so there will be a forum for discussing ethical issues related to scientific and technological progress. But I'm worried it could be too late to make a difference.

I have been praying to God about this because it feels as though the human race is speedily heading for total disaster. Surely some major catastrophes aren't too far off, such is the recklessness of technology companies which are seemingly not being constrained by politicians and governments.

I don't feel at all excited about all of this technological 'progress'. There is a global race for technological dominance but the potentially disastrous effects of this ongoing industrial revolution are not being properly considered. How can they be when everything is happening so quickly?

Obviously, God is in control and knows what is going on. But I am despairing for myself and for all the sentient beings that will endure great suffering in the name of scientific progress. Technologists are in the process of connecting human brains to machines and cyborgs are in the process of becoming a reality.

Please, God, show me how I should react to everything that's happening. Should I persevere and try to build a church? Should I commit my life to following Christianity? Should I kill myself? Or should I move out of London?

I desperately, desperately want God to give me a passage to safety, a way to escape from the terrifying future which is emerging so quickly. Please, God, save me from this disastrous state of affairs. I would much rather die than live through the times I see coming. Please, God, help me to develop a plan and a way to escape the rapidly approaching torment. Please be merciful to me, Lord, and to the human race.

Remember, Lord, how terrible it is for us humans to suffer torture. Please don't do it to me, and to us, Lord. Should I pray to Jesus? It's so hard not having a spiritual home. I have never looked at the future and dreaded it so much.

Lord, all I want is to experience simple joy and peace. I don't covet power or money, I just want the comfort of a deep love that leaves no room for fear. What must I do, Lord, in order for You to end my suffering? I beg of You, Lord, be merciful. Please, God, be merciful.

IX

2020

114

THE GREAT VACUOUSNESS OF ALL
THAT I AM AND EVER WILL BE

24th January 2020

The question of why there is something rather than nothing – why anything exists at all – is very confusing to me. However, I realise that confusion is just an energetic state; it's perfectly possible that to You (God) there is no mystery. It is a strange thing being a creature, knowing that You are controlling my every thought, word, deed, and bodily process, and that I don't exist as a free creature, despite having lived for 37 years as Steven Colborne.

When I have a conversation with someone, what is really happening is that You are talking with Yourself. One puppet is talking to another puppet. This is the ultimate truth. I can understand why You might find this frustrating – never having another free creature with whom to interact, and having to live without genuine free interaction for all eternity.

Of course, that is a very human perspective, and it's quite possible that You experience perfect bliss at all times, and that it is only Your puppets (Your creatures) that experience suffering. I have speculated in my book *God's Grand Game* that perhaps on one level You experience everything that we experience, but on another level, You remain free from, and distinct from, our suffering. I can only speculate, because my perception and understanding are limited — I am in a kind of creaturely prison where things are deeply mysterious.

There is nothing I could go through, gain, or achieve, that would add anything to what You already know — that could surprise You or alter Your understanding of things. This is one of the characteristics of Your "aloneness" and "oneness" — You are already complete, whether this is a joyful thing or not. There is nothing new under the sun (or, indeed, anywhere in existence). Even these words that I am now sharing are intrinsically meaningless, as everything is.

115

SOME WORDS ABOUT GOD

16th March 2020

God is awesome, majestic, wonderful, glorious, wise, humorous, grand, mysterious, mighty, and greatly to be feared.

God is masterful in His creativity, He's a friend to the poor in spirit, He's the solution to every problem, the answer to every question, the peace in the midst of the chaos, the cure for every ailment.

God is the strong and fearless creator of the Universe, sovereign over every event, creating confusion and then bringing a solution, knocking you down so He can raise you back up, giving you a punishing depression and then turning it into ecstatic elation, creating great suffering and then bringing relief and healing.

God did not create the Universe at some time in the past and then sit back and watch it unfold from a distance, He is a living and omnipresent God who is unfolding every event in this single eternal moment, which is not ontologically distinct from Him.

God is not the author of only some events, but is actively unfolding all events. God is not in competition with an enemy, He is all-powerful and nothing ever happens that He does not actively bring about.

There is not an atom anywhere in existence which is outside of God's sovereign present moment control.

These words about God are true.

116

WHY DOES GOD PUNISH DREADFULLY, WHEN JESUS TEACHES FORGIVENESS?

23rd April 2020

I re-read the book of Revelation today. It seems to me that the teachings of Jesus — who emphasised love of neighbour, love of God, and forgiveness of our enemies — are at odds with the way God's character is depicted in the Bible.

The Book of Revelation is absolutely terrifying in respect of some of the things it says God will do to sentient beings in the future, such as sending plagues, a bottomless pit, torturing for 1000 years, throwing people into a lake of fire, killing all ocean life, etc.

And, of course, in the Old Testament, God is believed to have obliterated the human race in a great flood, as well as punishing nations on countless occasions by sending plagues and droughts, or through violent wars. If you believe God is sovereign over all events, as I certainly do, then divine punishment seems very cruel and unnecessary, because God is punishing people for things they have done which He has actively caused them to do.

How can the character of God and the character of Jesus be so different, when Jesus is supposedly God? Why can't God forgive people in the way Jesus teaches humans they must? I'm really struggling to accept the Biblical presentation of a God who is unspeakably cruel. It just doesn't make sense.

It seems that the Biblical justification for God's severe punishment is His supposed anger over sin. We are all apparently guilty because of something that Adam and Eve did long before we were born, and regardless of whether we do our best to be kind and loving people during our lives on Earth. Christian evangelists will rebuke everyone without exception, claiming that because we have all slipped up at least once in our lives, we do not meet God's high standard of holiness and purity, and this makes us deserving of hell. Really?

It's perfectly possible that God might torment His creatures dreadfully and in the ways we read about in the book of Revelation. But if God is all-powerful, and His natural state is one of peace (as I have argued it likely is in my essay about Covid-19), then it doesn't really make sense that He would be so angry as to punish with the kind of gruelling severity described in the Bible.

Some Christians reading this will no doubt take the standpoint that whatever is in the Bible, we must believe without question. Of course, Christians disagree on pretty much every issue of Biblical theology there is, so "believing the Bible" is in no way black and white. I understand that those Christians who elevate the authority of the Bible do so out of a fear of God, and I respect that — reading the Bible definitely creates great fear, there is no doubt about it.

But I have found myself asking this important question, which I also invite readers to consider: Which am I more happy to call into question, the Christian worldview (as expounded in the Bible), or God Himself, as I believe Him to be? My way of dealing with this problem will be to think through the issues with an open mind and pray about the issues I have discussed here, and I hope God will enlighten me as to the Truth of the matter, whatever it is.

IS CHRISTIANITY TRUE?

4th May 2020

For the purposes of this article, I take for granted a belief in the perspective of monotheism. Arguments for the existence of God are not the focus of this article, but I have discussed this matter extensively elsewhere on this blog and in my books. This article is intended to help believers in a single God to consider whether or not they should embrace Christianity.

Introduction: Three Possibilities

When considering whether or not to accept the Christian worldview, there are only three logical possibilities. I will list the three possibilities and then elaborate on the content of each of the statements.

1) We have free will and therefore an orthodox Biblical Christian worldview makes sense of reality

2) God is in control of all events (we do not have free will) and double predestination is true

3) God is in control of all events (we do not have free will) and the Christian worldview must be called into question

Statement One

Let us begin with the first statement. If we have free will, then it makes sense that we might be sinners who are potentially rebelling against God, and are potentially guilty of certain things, and are potentially deserving of judgement and punishment. Jesus may well have atoned for the sins which we have freely committed, and we may well have a free choice as to whether or not to believe in Jesus and obey His teaching.

It is clear that the idea of free will is central to all of the key Christian doctrines I have just described, and if we have free will, I for one would be satisfied that the Christian worldview makes sense of reality and should be pursued.

There will be some who could happily stop reading at this point, but for the deep thinkers among you, please read on, because what I have to say is important.

The Argument Against Free Will

I am convinced that we don't have free will, for the reasons I have explained countless times in my previous written works. I have argued against free will using numerous examples, and discussing the problem from a range of different angles. It would take up too much space for me to repeat all of my arguments here, but I will just state summarily that my view is that God is omnipresent and the animator of everything that happens in existence. God's boundlessness means that there is nothing outside the being of God and so there is literally no room for freedom from God, or free will.

If you don't understand this argument and would like to hear me elaborate upon it further, please do read my book *God's Grand Game*, or check out my *Deep Thoughts About God* video series, because this argument is central to my understanding of reality.

I should mention, at this point, that there are Christians who attempt to argue that it is simultaneously true that God is sovereign over all events and that we have free will (see, for instance, the chapters on Compatibilism, Open Theism, Calvinism and Molinism in *God's Grand Game*). But my argument in relation to all of these philosophies is that they do not make sense, because it is logically impossible for God to be sovereign over all events and at the same time for human beings to have free will.

Actually, it's quite common for orthodox Bible-believing Christians to implicitly acknowledge that they don't have free will. For instance, whenever a Christian prays for God to plant them in a great church, or to bless their marriage or their ministry, or to make their job interview go well, or to heal their sickness, they are acknowledging God's sovereign control over every aspect of their lives (this argument is expounded further in *God's Grand Game*). The fact that some believers pray in this way and simultaneously argue that they have free will represents a clear contradiction in their thinking.

Statement Two: Double Predestination

Now, let us look at Point 2. Double predestination is a doctrine embraced by some Calvinists that acknowledges God's sovereignty over all events. The view is that God predestines some people to be believers in Christ, even before they are born, and others to be damned, even before they are born.

This perspective is certainly a possibility, in that God could logically unfold events in this way, seeing as He is in perfect control of everything that happens, and is responsible to no one. But if God is really like this – that even before He has created a human being He decides that their destiny will be eternal punishment – there is no denying that such a perspective would make God an incredibly cruel being. So we are forced to consider whether it's likely that God is cruel in this way.

As I argued in my article entitled *Life: Tragedy or Comedy?* it is possible that God is angry for certain reasons (although, I might add, not because of sin; if He is sovereign over all events then He is the cause of all so-called sin, and why would He cause sin in order to make Himself angry?). God may be angry due to a kind of loneliness, or the fact that His existence will never have an ending (I have elaborated on these examples in *God's Grand Game*).

If God suffers terribly, this might be a justification for double predestination, because God might want to appease His anger and do so through tormenting His creatures. I would say, however, that it's not clear to me why even if God is angry He would necessarily need to express His anger by making His creatures suffer terribly. In any case, I think it's more likely that God's natural state is perfect bliss (see my essay entitled *God and Suffering: A Covid-19 Theology*) and so this would, at least in my view, leave Him without motive or justification for damning human beings.

Statement Three: The Christian Worldview must be Questioned

The final option of the three I presented is that God is in control of all events and therefore the Christian worldview doesn't reflect reality. The argument is quite simple: If God is in control of our thoughts, words, and actions, then central Christian doctrines such as sin, salvation, judgement, etc — which all depend on free will — don't make sense.

At this point, I believe it's wise to take a step back and look at the bigger picture. Christianity is a religion that has been around on a single planet for around two thousand years. Scientists estimate that the universe is around fourteen billion years old, and that billions of planets exist. I'm not one to blindly believe the statistics of scientists, but when I gaze out into the night sky I have a sense that such incredible vastness is possible.

Even if we confine our considerations only to Planet Earth, there are billions of human beings who have lived and died without encountering the Christian worldview (unless, of course, all of these people encountered Jesus in a dream, or a vision, or a near death experience, or such like). There are also the billions of people who feel they are serving God in accordance with non-Christian religions, such as Islam, Sikhism, and the Bahá'í Faith, for example. Can it really be the case that all of these billions of lives are relatively unimportant to

God, because these people did not embrace Jesus as Lord and Saviour and lead a Christian life?

An alternative perspective, which embraces the idea of God's sovereignty over the entirety of creation, is that Christianity should be seen as one great religion among many. According to this worldview, Jesus is an immensely important person in God's Grand Game, and no doubt an astonishing teacher and healer. But what the New Testament teaches about sin and judgment cannot make sense in a world where we don't have free will. Instead, Jesus could be considered a great prophet, as Muslims argue he is, but possibly not the only way to have peace with God.

Conclusion

I will leave readers with these questions to consider:

Is there a positive role for every human being in God's plan? Does the doctrine of hell make sense in light of God's sovereignty over all events? And, of course, the question it all hinges upon — do we really have free will?

I do believe that the three options presented in this article are a logical way of looking at the problem of whether or not Christianity is true and should be embraced wholeheartedly.

118

HEARING FROM GOD

16th May 2020

What do you do if God tells you something that is in direct contradiction with something that's taught in the Bible? The Christian might say, "God will *never* tell you anything that contradicts Biblical theology." To take this position is to elevate the Bible above the free will of God. Is it not true that God is an entirely free being without restrictions, and can do whatever He pleases, even if what He says or does contradicts what is taught in the Bible?

I suppose the Christian might argue that God *could* contradict the Bible, but He never *would*. Well, the testimony of many people from non-Christian religions would appear to provide evidence against such a position. Or is the Truth that God *only* speaks to orthodox Christians, and only does so in accordance with Biblical theology? This would mean that anyone else who claims they have heard from God is deluded;

even if that number amounts to millions, or even billions of people.

There are only two alternative explanations that I can imagine, from a Christian standpoint. The first is that satan is controlling the thoughts of every person who feels they hear from God in a way that is contrary to orthodox Biblical theology. The other is that God is lying to anyone who hears from Him in such a way, perhaps as part of His plan to damn the majority of human beings in line with the doctrine of double predestination.

The only other conclusion I can envisage is that God truly does speak to people in a way that is contrary to orthodox Biblical theology, because He has a plan for their lives that is outside of the Christian faith. This might be true if God has a positive and meaningful plan for every human being; but this is a perspective that cannot be justified according to orthodox Christianity, which paints Christianity as an exclusivist religion, where one is either saved in accordance with Biblical theology, or damned.

119

A GUIDE FOR AGNOSTICS

16th May 2020

In this article, I would like to offer a six point thought process that it is logical to go through when trying to discern whether or not embracing Christianity is a wise idea. I hope the guide will help someone who is currently agnostic but is exploring (or considering exploring) the Christian faith.

Before we begin, I would like to note my own perspective, which is that I find excellent arguments for embracing Christianity, and also excellent arguments as to why Christianity doesn't make sense. Some of the arguments for and against will come out in this article, but for agnostics who want to go deeper, I recommend reading my essay *An Almighty Predicament*.

Without further ado, I will state the six aforementioned considerations, with some personal reflections on each consideration under each heading.

Should I Become a Christian?

Six key considerations

1) In order to have a gospel, you have to have some bad news.

If salvation means anything, we must need to be saved from something. So there must be bad news from which human beings might need to be saved. The bad news creates the problem which the good news (the gospel) remedies.

2) Is there really bad news, or is this a Christian fabrication?

Christians locate the bad news in the fall of man, and sin — ideas found in the Bible. But these are concepts which are questionable in light of a sovereign and omnipresent God, for I believe that God's boundlessness leaves no room for freedom from God, or free will.

The Christian doctrines of the fall of man and sin depend on free will. If sin is a part of God's will, then surely it is not something that angers God, because He has chosen to manifest it. If sin angers God, then logically, He could simply choose not to create sin. So punishment for sin wouldn't really make sense if there is a God who is in control of all things.

An alternative but related viewpoint (if we acknowledge the idea of sin), is that God creates sin with the specific purpose of punishing sinners, as part of some grand plan for humankind. This view paints a picture of an unspeakably and arbitrarily cruel God, which I for one find hard to accept.

Christians who believe in 'double predestination' hold this kind of view.

There are other, non-Biblical reasons why God might be angry and feel He must punish human beings which I have discussed in my book *God's Grand Game* in the chapter entitled 'The Agony of God'. Essentially, God might experience extreme frustration in relation to certain intrinsic limitations, such as being unable to ever create anything outside of Himself with which He could freely interact, and also having to live with the knowledge that His existence will never have an ending. These are not Christian ideas, but they are worth considering.

The only remaining possibility is that we do in fact have free will, and so we are guilty of original sin and also our own sins. This is the perspective from which the Christian worldview makes the most sense. However, it is my firm belief that an omnipresent God and human free will are logically contradictory and incompatible ideas, so readers are advised to think this problem through deeply for themselves.

3) If Jesus is God, then we must listen to Jesus on the subject.

God is omnipotent and has all authority, so we don't need to listen to Jesus unless He is either God in human form, as Christian orthodoxy argues He is, or he is instead a chosen prophet, or teacher, whose teachings are important.

4) So, is Jesus God?

Orthodox Christians argue that the Bible indisputably portrays Jesus as God. Muslims, on the other hand, argue that the text of the Bible has been corrupted in order to depict Jesus in a way that has distorted the reality of his prophethood, and made him into God. This, to Muslims, is deeply idolatrous. Messianic Jews believe Jesus is God, while many orthodox Jews disagree. And, of course, there are other religions with their own perspectives concerning who Jesus is.

5) God knows the Truth, so ask Him.

Some Christians insist that questions of theology can only be answered in the pages of the Bible. But is God greater than the Bible?

Because God is sovereign over all events, whenever a book is being written, there is a sense in which God is writing the book, even though He is doing so through one or more human beings under His control. Therefore, I believe it would be correct to say God has written every book that has ever existed, including the Bible but also the holy books of all non-Christian religions.

To me, therefore, it seems logical that God has authority over the Bible and all other books. This is important because it means that we can turn to God for understanding in relation to the doctrines and ideas presented in the Bible.

Asking God in prayer to reveal the Truth about Biblical teaching seems like the wisest thing to do when trying to discern matters of faith. We might pray for God to reveal which religion is true, and which teachings we should obey, as well as whether we should consider Jesus to be a prophet, or God in human form.

Surely, seeking answers directly from God in this way is an act of humility. My own view is that it is not a prideful rejection of the Bible to ask for God's help with discerning theological matters, but a logical way of discerning Truth. If God were to condemn people for asking Him for direction, that would seem to make God very cruel, and I have found no reason to believe He is.

6) Be obedient to God's response.

If you pray to God, perhaps He will tell you to follow Jesus, in which case that's what you must do. Perhaps God won't answer you at all, in which case I suggest you keep searching and asking. Or perhaps God will direct you to understand Jesus as a prophet, but not God, or will direct you along some other spiritual path.

It's obvious to me that God has created every religion, and even every non-religious perspective. He has created every human being in exactly the way He wanted, with all their myriad different beliefs. It seems to me that prayer, therefore, is the most logical way of attempting to discern Truth, and is the best method we have for coming to an understanding of which spiritual path we should follow.

Even readers who are unsure about whether or not a God even exists should consider saying a prayer to ask for help. It is too important a matter not to at least employ a little humility and see whether a prayer might work. There is really nothing to lose, other than a little pride perhaps, and pride is not virtuous for anyone, so I would definitely advise taking the risk and humbly asking God for guidance.

STREAM OF CONSCIOUSNESS

20th May 2020

The words of Jesus are absolutely compelling. But the fact that we do not have free will is absolutely compelling. God tells me one thing, which is very compelling. The Bible tells me something different, which is very compelling.

I have ambitions, through which I aim to alleviate suffering. Sometimes this seems noble. But then I am struck by the fear of acting in a way that is not totally submitted to Jesus.

The warnings of hellfire carry weight because the teaching of Jesus is so compelling. Yet when I commit to follow Jesus I soon remember that because we have no free will, the idea of sin, which is key to the teaching of Jesus, doesn't make sense,

So I think, the Bible must be wrong. I almost feel certain of this. I lay out logical thought processes which convince me that Biblical theology is illogical. But then I consider that the

Bible describes everlasting torment for those who don't believe.

I consider everlasting torment and how cruel it would make God. Yet I also know there is great joy in following Jesus. But how can God punish people in hell for acts that He, by His sovereign will, has caused them to do?

So I consider God wouldn't be so cruel as to send people to hell. But then this is to deny the teaching of Jesus, who claims to be God. And yet Jesus seems kind, which makes me think God must be merciful. But then I consider hell, and that God is willing to show no mercy to some, according to Scripture.

But all I have to do is put my faith in Jesus to avoid damnation? No, for I must also pick up my cross and follow Him, which could involve great suffering, even martyrdom. But surely this is preferable to eternal punishment. All the martyrs of the past chose worldly suffering over eternal suffering.

But then there are martyrs for Islam as well as Christianity. How am I to make sense of that? I consider this and reflect that surely God has a role for every human being, not just those who follow Jesus, and He unfolds the lives of Muslims and atheists, as well as Christians.

Then I consider the doctrine of double predestination, and how it is the only way to understand Christianity if God is sovereign over all events. But it is such a cruel doctrine, and I don't want to accept that God would be cruel.

Here lies Martin Elginbrod
Have mercy on my soul Lord God
As I would do were I Lord God
And ye were Martin Elginbrod

Are all Christians as afraid of God as I am? Why is God so frightening if He's a loving God?

The Bible speaks of God's wrath over sin. Why then, does He not just unfold a universe without sin? If hell exists, and God is sovereign, He must choose to damn people. Even though He has been in control of everything they've ever done.

But the Christian will say, we DO have free will. No, Christian, we don't. When you pray to God, Christian, you ask Him for things that prove that you know He is in control of your life in its entirety. You pray for Him to bless your marriage, your children, your spiritual life, your job. And then you claim at the same time you have free will? Christian, you are in error. You say 'God is in control' because that comforts you, but then you say 'We have free will' because the Bible teaches sin. This is a logical contradiction at the very heart of the Christian faith, which I cannot ignore.

But maybe I *should* ignore this contradiction, and adopt the position of Pascal and his wager? Even if Christianity makes no sense at all, maybe I should just do my best to live in accordance with Biblical theology? Yes, that's what I should do. But then, despite my prayers for peace and clarity, the free will problem comes up again, and I am certain that we don't have free will.

Look, it's obvious. God's being is boundless. He is omnipresent. There is not a place where the being of God ends and freedom from God begins. There is nothing outside of God's control. I know this to be true. We do not have free will.

The solid truth that we do not have free will is a knock down argument against Christianity, isn't it? Or perhaps, in line with Pascal's wager, I must ignore this truth and believe the gospel, because that is my only chance of avoiding hellfire.

Yes, that's it. I must obey Jesus. The words of Jesus are so compelling. "I am the way, the truth, and the life" "I am the light of the world" "I am the bread of life" "The only way to the Father is through the Son".

Well, either these claims of Jesus must be true, or they aren't. They are incredibly persuasive, especially in the context of the whole Bible. But maybe those people who compiled the Bible did so in such a way as to make it as convincing as possible. Maybe they left out many contradictory and troublesome writings, and put together something theologically cohesive just to make the argument for Christianity as compelling as possible. Bart Ehrman and others have studied the Bible in incredible depth, and come to the conclusion that it is not trustworthy, so why shouldn't I agree with them?

Oh gosh, Jesus said 'He who puts his hand to the plough and looks back is not fit for the Kingdom of God', that means I can't be fit, because of these thoughts that I am having that are doubting the veracity of the Christian faith. But God is controlling these thoughts, so there's nothing I can do about it.

I suppose God might want to damn me. Then there's nothing I can do. Does God want to damn me because I can't make up my mind about Christianity? But He is the one who is causing me to not make up my mind, so why doesn't He just make me make up my mind?

Perhaps all of this questioning is a demonstration of my fear of God, and my love of Truth, which would be something that would please God. Perhaps the most important thing in life is to be kind, to do good, and to love my my neighbour as myself. Then it doesn't seem so important that everything I do is in line with Biblical theology, I just have to love people.

Didn't Jesus say that the whole of the law is to love God and love my neighbour? I think I do love God and love my neighbour, so maybe I am safe. But the Christian would say loving God means loving the Christian God, and loving the Christian God means being submitted to Jesus, and being submitted to Jesus means taking up my cross and following Him, and therefore I don't think I am fully submitted to Jesus, otherwise I wouldn't be thinking like this.

Actually, come to think of it, do I even know Jesus? In the past I have been so immersed in Christian life in a very genuine way. I have sung songs about my love of Jesus in a very genuine way. I have preached about Jesus to others in a very genuine way.

Perhaps I am a backslider, but I hate that term, because it doesn't appreciate my struggle. I am not backsliding, I am trying to establish TRUTH. But yes, there it is again, Jesus is the way, the TRUTH and the life, so I must follow Him.

But actually, so what if Jesus said He is the truth? If someone else says they are the truth, then should I follow them? Why are Jesus' words to be believed over and above anyone else?

Well, the Christian would say, because Jesus is God. Well that settles things, doesn't it? If Jesus is God then He has all authority. But the Muslims claim that calling Jesus God is the worst sin there is. There are a billion Muslims who believe this. So are these Muslims going to hell? Or are all Christians going to hell, because claiming God has a son is blasphemy? Muslims believe this! What if they are right?

If the Muslims are correct and Jesus is a prophet, then maybe Christians should be more humble. Perhaps if Christians were to embrace Jesus as a prophet, then common ground could be found among Muslims and Christians. Perhaps the divinity of Jesus is a fabrication.

But there are compelling scriptures in the Bible that demonstrate Jesus really did claim to be God, so how are we to know? Perhaps we cannot know for sure, and that is why we have to have faith. So I suppose I must put my faith in Jesus, and do my best to wholeheartedly follow Him. But I am not in control of whether I do that or not, it is God who controls that.

My goodness, my Christian readers are going to think I am an awful person for wrestling so much about things which they find relatively easy. The scripture comes to mind about the man who built his house on the sand, it had no foundations. I suppose that's what my Christian readers will think of me — Steven is such an idiot because he can't just put his faith in Jesus and make the commitment.

But Christian, God is in control of my life, I have no choice in the matter! Maybe some Christian readers think that's a cheap cop out. But God know the truth of the matter, which is that I am being completely honest.

I get excited when I think about my plans for the future. But I don't know whether my plans line up properly with Biblical theology. Maybe it's selfish to have plans and dreams. But don't they come from God? Doesn't every thought we have come from God? Of course it does. But this means God must want me to be struggling with all these issues.

Perhaps God does want me to struggle with these issues, because He is refining my character and teaching me about Christianity through my struggles. Yes, that would make sense. That is a comforting thought, that all of this might be part of God's plan, and that He doesn't hate me.

Why would God hate me? He has made me exactly the way I am.

I'm so tired of this struggle. Sometimes I enjoy the struggle, sometimes I hate it. I love my writing, because I think it contains important and deep insights. But then the Christian might say that any book which doesn't reflect submission to Jesus is pointless. Maybe I should burn every copy of every book I have written that doesn't demonstrate submission to Jesus?

But hang on, another thought. Within Christianity there are countless denominations and countless viewpoints. Isn't Roman Catholicism the only true faith? That's what Roman Catholics believe. But then Roman Catholics often talk about how everyone will be saved eventually, perhaps after a spell of purification in purgatory. Perhaps I should commit to Catholicism because it's the largest Christian denomination... can all those Catholics really be wrong?

But the idea of the Pope! All those fancy robes and the way people seem to worship him. Protestant Christians hate all that. It certainly doesn't seem to line up with the teaching of Jesus.

Which reminds me, I haven't taken communion for ages. Maybe some Christian readers will think that's another reason why I'm struggling. Perhaps my Anglican readers would think that, because communion is a big part of the way they practice Christianity.

But then my friends in Hillsong church barely ever take communion, and they don't think it's important to do so regularly, although they do it once a month or once every two months. They are much more relaxed about it than the Anglicans.

I think some Christians sin all week long, and then they take communion on a Sunday and say a few prayers, and thereby feel they are cleansed from their sins, which they then go off and commit again. Well, perhaps this is okay? Or are they living a lie?

This feels good to be getting my thoughts out in the open. But it hasn't brought me any closer to settling my predicament. Do I embrace Christianity or don't I?

I will have to make a decision soon, because God surely hates indecision. Even though He is causing my indecision, I am 100% certain of that.

Look, I must be taking all of this way too seriously. 99% of the people on the planet don't care at all about these things. They just get on with their lives. Agonising over Christianity in this way must make me very strange. But actually, it doesn't feel strange because it is honest. And anyway, the Bible talks about entering through the narrow gate, which leads me to think only a small number of people will be saved, so all those people who are getting on with their lives are going to end up in hell anyway.

But actually, maybe it's the case that even if someone has lived a life of sin, entirely outside of the Christian faith, but then on their deathbed confesses Jesus, they will go to heaven and everything will be fine for them? God could certainly choose for that to happen. God can do whatever He pleases. Maybe to God, someone who lives their entire life in sin but then repents on their deathbed, is just as valuable as someone who tries to do good works for their entire life.

Protestants argue that works are not important, but are a natural sign of true faith. Roman Catholics, on the other hand, argue that works are crucial. So either millions of Catholics are wrong, or millions of Protestants are wrong. So how am I to know which denomination to choose?

Maybe I need to find a spiritual guru to support me with these struggles. I tried talking to a priest in Wandsworth about panentheism but he didn't say anything helpful. I think most of the people in the Anglican church who are priests don't even consider half the things that I do. Not that I should be judging them.

I think about my relationships, and how they have always been much better when I have been following Jesus. There is always a joy when one feels one is serving the Lord. When I'm serving Jesus I become more aware that I must honour my father and mother. Well, my mother passed away long ago, but I become more aware that I should honour my father. It's easy to forgive others when one is conscious of God's forgiveness.

Actually, that's quite reassuring. Maybe God is forgiving. But then why does He damn people to hell?

✲ 121 ✲

A CONVERSATION WITH SANDRA

5th June 2020

What follows is a made-up dialogue between myself and my fictional Christian friend, 'Sandra'. I hope that after reading it you will understand my predicament surrounding the Christian faith a little more clearly.

Sandra:

I've got to be honest with you, Steven. I've felt myself backsliding recently. I don't read the Bible as much as I used to and I've only been to church once in the last two months. The thing is, I feel so depressed without God.

Steven:

I can understand your frustration. However, the reality of God is that He doesn't come and go, so you mustn't use that phrase 'without God'. Just as God was in control of your life when you were devotedly reading the Bible, He is still in control of your life now, only in a different way. The guilt that you feel is also from God – it's just a different mode of mind under His control. So rest assured that everything you're going through is part of God's will for your life.

Sandra:

Well, thanks Steven. That is a comforting thought. But what makes you think God is in control of every area of my life? Are you saying I don't have free will? I couldn't accept that, because the Bible describes me as a fallen sinner in need of salvation. I *have* walked away from God, and that is why I'm hurting.

Steven:

I appreciate that you're hurting right now, but you might find some consolation by looking at things in a slightly different way. I would like to ask you to reflect deeply on two questions: *What is God?* and *Where is God?*

When I deeply considered the answers to these questions myself, I realised that God must be pure spirit without boundaries. It didn't make sense to me that there could be limits to the extent of God's being, as when I examined my own consciousness, I intuited that it was something free from any kind of form or container. If there are no limits to my own consciousness, that means that there is only one consciousness. I equate that one consciousness with God.

Sandra:

It sounds to me as though you're saying you are God!

Steven:

Well, I believe there is a sense in which my consciousness is the same as God's consciousness, that's true. However, my consciousness is experienced through the vessel of the body and its five senses, whereas God has no such limitations, and I believe He is most likely aware of all that exists, all of the time. So there is a distinction between creaturely consciousness and God consciousness. We experience things in the human dimension of reality, while God experiences things in a more deep and vibrant way in the ultimate dimension.

Sandra:

How can you claim to know what God experiences?

Steven:

I cannot, for sure. But what gave me confidence in this perspective was firstly examining my own consciousness and its apparent boundlessness, and secondly an experience I had when meditating deeply some years ago, when I felt my bodily form dissolve into a feeling of expansive bliss. The blissful feeling was one of a far greater wholeness and completeness than I have ever experienced in my regular waking state, and so this led me to speculate that God experiences this kind of blissful awareness at all times.

Sandra:

But that was just an experience you had. How is it linked to God?

Steven:

I would refer once again to my understanding of consciousness as being boundless. The boundlessness of existence
means that everything that exists is a part of God. So there is
a sense in which I believe God is my 'higher self'. If I were to
die right now, or meditate deeply, I might once again connect
with the deeper awareness and pure bliss that I believe is the
essence of God.

Sandra:

You seem to be describing God as an impersonal feeling. The
Bible teaches that God is personal. What would you have to
say about that?

Steven:

I believe God is personal, in that He is able to give creatures a
feeling of separateness from Him and communicate with
them directly by talking to their minds. He can make us feel
isolated and identified with our human bodies and He can
also talk to us as though He is a separate being. Again, this is
because we are experiencing things through the senses.

Think of it this way. God is the great 'I AM'. He is all that
exists. Think of Him as like an infinitely large oak tree, and
think of us as the branches on the tree. God's life force flows
through the whole tree, but each branch has a kind of independent existence, even though really it is part of the tree. It's
an imperfect analogy, but I believe it captures something of
our relationship with God.

Sandra:

So we're simultaneously part of God but also experience things in a different way to Him?

Steven:

Yes, I think so. We could describe all of our activities as having a primary and secondary cause. Everything we do is orchestrated by God in the divine dimension, but we feel we are doing things ourselves in the human dimension. God is the primary cause, and we are the secondary cause. The important point is that there is no freedom in the secondary cause, because our actions are 100% under the control of the primary cause, which is God.

Sandra:

You believe I am 100% under God's control?

Steven:

Yes, and I believe you intuitively know this. When you pray a prayer along the lines of "God, please let my job interview go well" or "Lord, please bless my marriage", you are implicitly acknowledging that God is controlling the events of your life. If this wasn't the case, it wouldn't make sense to pray in such a way.

Sandra:

Actually, I believe God isn't in control of everything, but He can and does intervene sometimes.

Steven:

I appreciate that Christians often describe things in such a way. However, the omnipresence of God means that in reality, there is no room for free will. For there to be free will there would have to be separateness from God, but as I have already explained, I don't believe God's being has boundaries.

I notice that you haven't denied that you pray in a way that implicitly acknowledges God is controlling and unfolding all of the events of your life.

Sandra:

Well, I'll think about that. But can't God be omnipresent and we still have free will?

Steven:

No. The two ideas are logically contradictory. For anyone to act freely they would have to not be under God's control, but if everything that exists is contained within God, it logically follows that everything that exists must be under God's control.

Sandra:

I'm sorry, I can't accept this. The Bible says I'm a sinner in need of salvation. The Bible is the Word of God. Do you think you know better than God?

Steven:

All I do is try to be honest. I appreciate that the Christian gospel is very compelling. It compelled me to get baptised, and it compelled me to go out on the streets and evangelise. But during my time as a Christian I was never able to honestly resolve the free will predicament, because I believe it is an area of Christian theology which does not make sense.

Sandra:

Couldn't it be you that's incorrect, rather than the Bible?

Steven:

The Bible can be understood and interpreted in very many different ways, which is evidenced by the existence of multiple different denominations and schools of thought within Christianity. Christians have been disagreeing with one another for two thousand years. So it's difficult to sweepingly say whether the Bible is 'correct' or 'incorrect'.

Sandra:

Christians only disagree because human beings are imperfect. The Word of God is not imperfect, it is perfect.

Steven:

Well, in response to that argument, we have to look at hermeneutics, the way things come to have meaning. If you think about it, the contents of the Bible is lines and curly symbols impressed upon a white background. Lines and curly symbols upon a white background do not contain inherent meaning. What makes the written word meaningful is God bringing meaning to our minds as we read and reflect. Any single sentence can potentially be read and interpreted in an infinite number of ways.

Sandra:

So the Bible could mean anything? I disagree. Words are symbols that communicate.

Steven:

Have you considered the way in which words communicate? I don't wish to repeat myself, but let me offer an analogy. Have you ever had the experience of looking at the clouds in the sky, and seeing in them the form of a creature or an object? Then a few moments later you can see the same cloud formation as though it is a completely different and unrelated object. You can playfully imagine that the clouds are like paintings of different creatures or objects.

Sandra:

Yes, but you're talking about clouds, I'm talking about the Word of God.

Steven:

In terms of my hermeneutic, there is no difference. Just as clouds do not contain intrinsic meaning, neither do the lines and curly symbols on a page. The way we understand something depends on God bringing a particular understanding to our awareness, and there are no limits to the way in which God might do this.

Sandra:

So you think I could look at a cat and see a dog?

Steven:

Yes, I think that it's entirely possible for you to look at a cat and think 'dog'. I have tried a similar thought experiment, which I described and elaborated upon in my book *The Philosophy of a Mad Man*.

Sandra:

Why are you always plugging your books endlessly!?

Steven:

Because I believe they represent an important contribution to the fields of philosophy and theology.

Sandra:

Well, I believe Jesus over you any day. Jesus is God, you're just a human who calls himself a philosopher, which I think is a bit arrogant, actually.

Steven:

I respect your desire to honour God and live in accordance with Biblical theology. The Christian Scriptures are incredibly compelling, as is evidenced by their persistence over the last two millennia.

Sandra:

Exactly, two thousand years of the Christian faith must mean Christianity is the true religion of God.

Steven:

I don't accept that argument. Just because something persists for a long time doesn't make it true. It means it's appealing in some way, but not necessarily true.

Sandra:

How do you know that what you're saying is 'true'?

Steven:

I just talk and write honestly. That is all that I do.

Sandra:

Jesus is the way, the truth, and the life!

Steven:

Billions of people have a different understanding of Jesus, but I agree that the way in which Jesus spoke as presented in the New Testament is incredibly persuasive and powerful.

Sandra:

You just need to read the Bible more, surround yourself with God's people, get planted in a good church, pray honestly, and God will keep you in His Kingdom and give you eternal life.

Steven:

I wish it were so easy to dismiss the inconsistencies and apparent problems contained within Christian doctrine, but I find they are ever present in my mind, and to deny them would be like living a lie.

Sandra:

Living a lie? Jesus is the TRUTH!

Steven:

It is a difficult predicament. How can I be a Christian when, to me at least, the central doctrines and tenets of the Christian faith don't make sense?

Sandra:

The devil is liar! You're being deceived.

Steven:

Well, I would have to refer you back to my understanding that God is in control of everything that happens. If the devil exists, the devil is also under God's control. I don't believe I have any free choice about what I think and write, because I don't believe I have free will.

Sandra:

You're being unbiblical again.

Steven:

I'm just speaking honestly.

Sandra:

You are choosing to abandon the Christian faith.

Steven:

I'm simply speaking honestly about those areas of Christian doctrine which don't make sense to me. Have you heard of Pascal's Wager? Pascal put forth the idea that the wisest way to live is as a Christian, because if Christianity is true, the penalty for those who deny Christ is everlasting suffering, but if you become a Christian and Christianity is untrue, you have lost relatively little.

Sandra:

Exactly. It makes much more sense to be a Christian.

Steven:

From a certain perspective, it does. But there are also other perspectives which billions of people have, and also, when I have tried to live a committed Christian life in spite of my problems with Christian doctrine, I found it was almost impossible, as these problems were relevant to every church service, every house group meeting, every coffee with my Christian friends, and so on.

Sandra:

So you think you know better than Jesus?

Steven:

I honestly think that central Christian doctrines don't make sense. I believe God has given me the understanding that I have, that God is writing these words through me, and that God is the omnipresent creator, sustainer, and animator of all that exists.

Sandra:

Well then you're a heathen and you're going to hell.

Steven:

I hope that's not true. I would find it strange if God were to subject people to everlasting torment when they have done nothing freely to deserve such torment.

Sandra:

But you're denying Jesus, therefore you are dead in your sins, and so you do deserve hell.

Steven:

It's possible that there are other ways of looking at existence, and while I find the teaching of Jesus very compelling, I sometimes wonder whether Christianity might just be part of a bigger picture. I mean, two thousand years of Christian history might seem like a lot, but there are much older religions, and eternity is an incredibly long time and I would suggest that maybe in a few million or billion years God might be playing a different game.

Sandra:

You think this is a game?

Steven:

Only in the sense that I believe God is playfully unfolding all events in existence, and I believe He takes great pleasure in doing so.

Sandra:

The Bible says that God is angry at you because of your sin.

Steven:

Actually, I'm glad you mentioned that, because that gets right to the heart of my problems with Christianity. If we really had free will, then the idea of rebellion against God could potentially make sense. But in reality, I believe everything that happens does so by God's will, and therefore we don't freely 'sin'. Everything that we have ever done has been willed and directed by God, therefore the doctrines of sin, salvation, and judgement, make little sense.

Sandra:

Then we must have free will.

Steven:

I'm convinced that we don't, for the reasons I've stated. Are you freely beating your heart? Are you freely circulating your blood? Are you freely digesting your food? Are you freely creating your emotions? If you are freely doing all of these things, how are you doing them?

Sandra:

My brain controls my bodily processes.

Steven:

What is causing your brain to control your bodily processes?

Sandra:

My subconscious, I guess.

Steven:

What exactly is your subconscious?

Sandra:

It's the things my brain is doing that I'm not aware of.

Steven:

What is causing your brain to do those things?

Sandra:

My brain just does them, I suppose.

Steven:

Your brain 'just does them'?

Sandra:

Hmmm. Well, I suppose there must be some cause of my brain activity.

Steven:

Yes, there must. The way I see it is that it is a scientific myth that human experience and human consciousness are somehow the result of brain machines. It's obvious to me that God is animating all of the processes that we experience as part of our living state. This all ties into my arguments against free will. I wrote an article entitled "What is Causing Our Thoughts?" in which I explained that the idea that our thoughts are under the control of some kind of brain machine is absurd. I believe the truth is that our thoughts are brought about spontaneously by an animating force, which is God.

Sandra:

Now you're describing us as puppets, and I can't accept that.

Steven:

Puppetry is a very good analogy for what I believe is the truth. Why can't you accept it?

Sandra:

I'm not a robot!

Steven:

You're the one who was suggesting you are a kind of robot powered by your brain. I don't think we are robots at all, but we are certainly like puppets.

Sandra:

Okay, I need a break. But I'm not giving up on Jesus.

Steven:

As you wish. I respect your desire to follow Jesus, and I understand it very well. But out of curiosity, are you able to understand my arguments, and do you think they are valid?

ALSO BY STEVEN COLBORNE

God's Grand Game:
Divine Sovereignty and the Cosmic Playground
(Tealight Books, 2019)

The Philosophy of a Mad Man
(Tealight Books, 2019)

An Almighty Predicament:
A Discourse on the Arguments For and Against Christianity
(Tealight Books, 2019)

Ultimate Truth: God Beyond Religion
(SilverWood Books, 2013)

The Only Question You Ever Need Ask
(Tealight Books, 2019)

A Collection of Essays by Steven Colborne
(Tealight Books, 2020)

Big Ideas from Ancient Greece
(Tealight Books 2019)

CONTACT DETAILS AND WEBSITES

Contact Steven:
riversofchange@gmail.com

Visit Steven online:
www.stevencolborne.com
www.perfectchaos.blog

Social Media:
www.youtube.com/c/stevencolborne
www.facebook.com/StevenColborneAuthor
www.instagram.com/stevencolborne
www.twitter.com/stevencolborne

Printed in Poland
by Amazon Fulfillment
Poland Sp. z o.o., Wrocław